D0844370

AVICENNA

(IBN SINA)

Muslim Physician and Philosopher
of the Eleventh Century

Great Muslim Philosophers and Scientists of the Middle Ages™

AVICENNA
(IBN SINA)

Muslim Physician and Philosopher
of the Eleventh Century

Aisha Khan

The Rosen Publishing Group, Inc., New York

To my darling Saamrya

Published in 2006 by The Rosen Publishing Group, Inc.
29 East 21st Street, New York, NY 10010

First Edition

Library of Congress Cataloging-in-Publication Data

Khan, Aisha.
Avicenna (Ibn Sina): Muslim physician and philosopher of the eleventh century/Aisha Khan.—1st ed.
        p. cm.—(Great Muslim philosophers and scientists of the Middle Ages)
Includes bibliographical references and index.
ISBN 1-4042-0509-8 (library binding)
1. Avicenna, 980–1037. 2. Philosophy, Medieval. 3. Philosophy, Islamic.
4. Physicians—Islamic Empire—Biography. 5. Muslim physicians—
Islamic Empire—Biography.
I. Title. II. Series.

B751.Z7K48 2006
181'.5—dc22

                                                                2005015787

Manufactured in the United States of America

On the cover: This undated portrait of Avicenna (Ibn Sina, 980–1037) hangs in the Bibliotheque de la Faculte de Medecine, in Paris, France.

CONTENTS

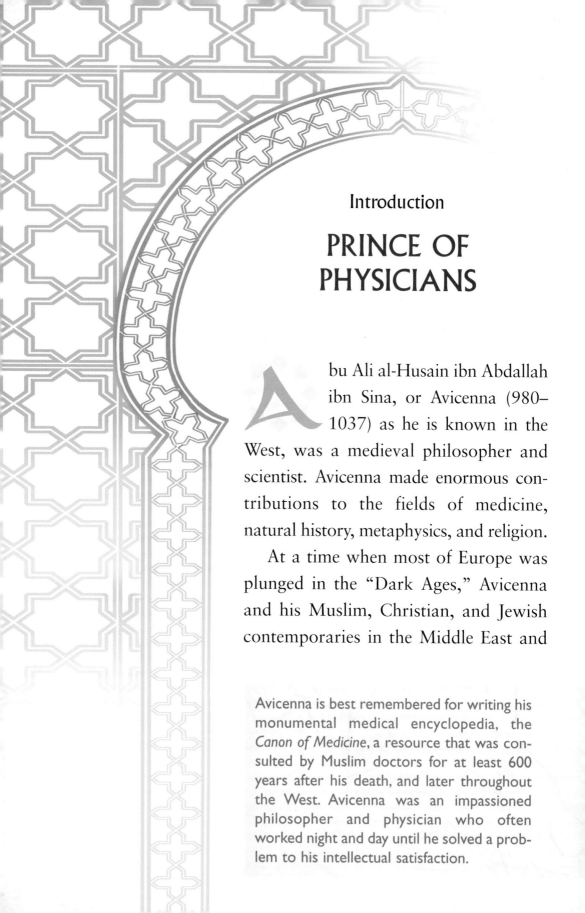

Introduction

PRINCE OF PHYSICIANS

bu Ali al-Husain ibn Abdallah ibn Sina, or Avicenna (980–1037) as he is known in the West, was a medieval philosopher and scientist. Avicenna made enormous contributions to the fields of medicine, natural history, metaphysics, and religion.

At a time when most of Europe was plunged in the "Dark Ages," Avicenna and his Muslim, Christian, and Jewish contemporaries in the Middle East and

Avicenna is best remembered for writing his monumental medical encyclopedia, the *Canon of Medicine*, a resource that was consulted by Muslim doctors for at least 600 years after his death, and later throughout the West. Avicenna was an impassioned philosopher and physician who often worked night and day until he solved a problem to his intellectual satisfaction.

the Muslim-ruled lands of Spain (al-Andalus) were on an extraordinary mission of learning and discovery.

Inspired by their reading of great Greek philosophers such as Plato (428–348 BC) and Aristotle (384–322 BC), and the ancient writings of physicians such as Hippocrates (460-377 BC) and Galen (129–199), these scholars tried to improve and apply their newfound knowledge to their own time and religious context.

Avicenna was born in the Persian-speaking region of central Asia. At the time, Baghdad, the capital of the Muslim world, was an unparalleled center of learning. This was the golden age of Islam, a period when rulers funded the arts and sciences, and philosophers, artists, architects, and poets of all religions and ethnicities created a unique culture whose legacy is still cherished today.

In today's world, Avicenna would have been called a prodigy—he had outpaced his teachers by the time he was fourteen years of age, and was practicing medicine by the age of sixteen. He wrote his first book at twenty-one.

As was the custom of the times, Avicenna sought royal patrons for his endeavors; as a result, he served sultans by day and pursued his personal scholarly interests by night.

Although Avicenna was curious about all branches of knowledge, his main concern was one that philosophers and scientists still ponder: the origin of the universe, and of life itself. A devout Muslim, Avicenna sought to reconcile the rational science he had learned from the Greeks with the Muslim belief in a single, supreme God. His aim was to prove scientifically, or at least through reason and logic, that God exists and is the creator of the world.

Avicenna's use of Aristotelian logic and his work on the concept of "being" opened the door for a rationalist study of religion. Avicenna influenced the work of later Christian philosophers such as St. Thomas Aquinas (1225–1274). Avicenna's reasoning and conclusions even anticipate the much later philosophical writings of great Enlightenment thinkers of the eighteenth century such as René Descartes (1586–1650) and Immanuel Kant (1724–1804).

But it is Avicenna's medical contributions for which he is most remembered. His monumental *Kitab al-Qanun fi al-Tibb*, known as the *Canon of Medicine*, is regarded as possibly the greatest medical work ever. This one-million-word encyclopedia not only systematically presented all known medical knowledge, it also incorporated Avicenna's experiences and discoveries as a practicing physician. The *Canon* was available in a Latin translation in Europe 100 years after Avicenna's death and continued to be used there for the next six centuries.

Avicenna's life was not one of mere book learning. As a practicing doctor and a political administrator, he incorporated his everyday observations into his work. His life was also marked by danger and intrigue. He was caught in

This illuminated seventeenth-century manuscript page is the first book of Avicenna's *Kitab al-Qanun fi al-Tibb* or *Canon of Medicine*. This first volume, sometimes called *al-Kulliyat*, was often copied and circulated separately from the rest of the *Canon* because it contained general medical principles. The *Canon of Medicine* was so popular in Europe after Avicenna's death that some sixty editions of all or parts of the work were translated from Arabic to Latin between 1100 and 1674. These translations were used in universities to help educate European doctors as part of their medical training.

conflicts between petty rulers, and he even spent some time in prison, where he continued to write. He died while traveling at the age of fifty-seven, fleeing an army that had overrun his patron's kingdom.

Known as the prince of physicians, Avicenna was a true Renaissance man—a person with a wide range of interests and expertise—centuries before the Renaissance ushered in a new era of scientific learning.

He was a restless genius who wrote in his memoirs:

How I wish I could know who I am,
What it is in this world that I seek.

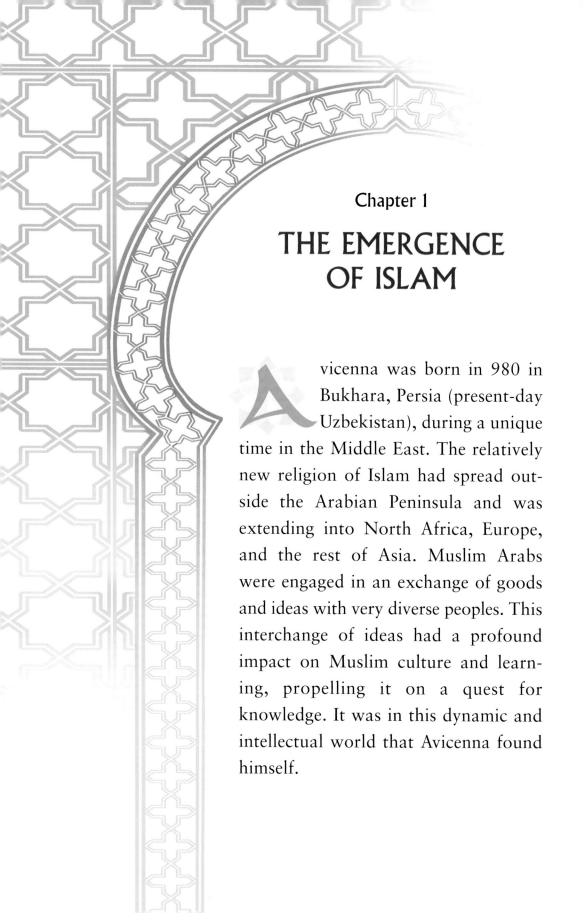

Chapter 1

THE EMERGENCE OF ISLAM

Avicenna was born in 980 in Bukhara, Persia (present-day Uzbekistan), during a unique time in the Middle East. The relatively new religion of Islam had spread outside the Arabian Peninsula and was extending into North Africa, Europe, and the rest of Asia. Muslim Arabs were engaged in an exchange of goods and ideas with very diverse peoples. This interchange of ideas had a profound impact on Muslim culture and learning, propelling it on a quest for knowledge. It was in this dynamic and intellectual world that Avicenna found himself.

This detail of a map featuring the eastern regions of Central Asia illustrates the reach of Islam throughout the area around the year AD 700. Islam had spread throughout the region from Arabia after Muhammad's death in 632. Today, Islam remains among the world's predominant religions along with Christianity and Judaism. There are more than 1 billion Muslims living and worshipping around the world.

A NEW FAITH

Three centuries before Avicenna's birth, Islam emerged in the early seventh century in western Arabia. A forty-year-old man named Muhammad (570–632), an illiterate merchant living in Mecca (Makkah), announced that the angel Gabriel had appeared before him to reveal the word of God.

The revelation was radically different from the beliefs and practices of the Arabs at the time. Muhammad called on them to abandon their multiple gods and idols and instead worship Allah, the one, true God.

Muhammad also said that life was only temporary, a short stop in the journey to an eternal life, which would come after death. He said there would be a day of judgment when all humanity would be resurrected and each person would have to answer to God. On that day, those who had led a good, honest life, remembering God and treating their fellow humans with charity and dignity would be rewarded with heaven. Sinners would be sent to hell.

Islam has many similarities with Judaism and Christianity, the two monotheistic faiths that preceded it. In fact, Muhammad (known to Muslims as the Prophet) preached that he was the last in a long line of prophets whom God had sent to show people the right path, starting with Adam, through Moses and Abraham, to Jesus. He urged Muslims to respect their fellow "People of the Book" (those who believe

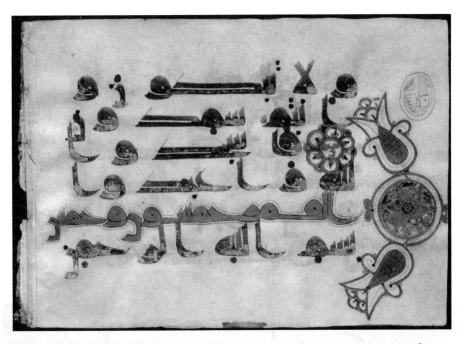

This ninth-century Tunisian manuscript page features a passage from the Qur'an (Koran). Muslims were among the first people to use paper (after the Egyptians and the Chinese). With the widespread use of paper to copy Qur'anic texts came the art of calligraphy, an expressive and elegant way of writing text. This manuscript uses the Kufic style, a type of angular and symmetrical calligraphy that was popular during Avicenna's lifetime. Kufic was developed by Muslims in the seventh century, and its use and popularity subsequently spread throughout the Muslim world.

in the Torah and the Bible) but said he had been chosen to deliver a new message because, over centuries, the teachings in the previous revelations had become distorted.

Muhammad received revelations for the next twenty years or so, until his death in 632. People memorized the revelations and wrote them on scraps of parchment and papyrus. After Muhammad's death, they were collected in a book called the Qur'an (also spelled "Koran") in a series of 114 chapters.

The powerful elite in Mecca, who made their living from the idol worship during the annual pilgrimages to the Kaaba shrine, were not pleased with Muhammad's message. Islam taught that everyone was equal, that status and respect were earned through good deeds and not inherited as a birthright. The elders turned violent, and Muhammad accepted the invitation from the people of Medina (or Madinah) to settle there in 622. The Muslim calendar begins from the year of this event, known as the *hijra*.

After many years of struggle and suppression, as well as three battles, Muhammad's teachings gained enough popularity that the elders of Mecca surrendered to his authority. He returned triumphant to his hometown in 630. By the time of his death two years later, Islam had spread throughout the Arabian Peninsula.

AFTER MUHAMMAD

With the death of the Prophet, the leading men in the Muslim community agreed on Muhammad's close friend and early convert Abu Bakr al-Asamm (573–634) as his successor, or caliph. Abu Bakr died of natural causes within two years and was succeeded in 634 by Umar ibn al-Khattab (586–644), a stern ruler who expanded the frontiers of Islam through military campaigns beyond the Arabian Peninsula. Battles under al-Khattab helped spread Islam farther west, into the Syrian and Egyptian provinces of the Byzantine Empire, and east into Iraq and Persia, which were part of the Sassanid dynasty. Both empires were long past their peaks and were weakened by epidemics, declining agriculture, and invasions. They were little match for the well-organized and motivated Arab forces. Both empires lost territory and were forced to pay annual tributes to the caliph.

The spread of Muslim rule was made easier because the vast majority of people cared little for who ruled over them. Although Muslims allowed the inhabitatants of the conquered lands to continue practicing their faiths, many converted to Islam. Others welcomed Muslim rule because their taxes were lowered. In addition, Muslim converts who learned Arabic had other decreased financial burdens and the potential of obtaining a position within the new administration.

In Mecca, however, tensions between the dominant tribes were growing. The third caliph, Uthman ibn Affan (574–656), was accused of giving jobs to his own clan. A group emerged that claimed Ali ibn Abi Talib (600–661), a cousin and son-in-law of Muhammad, should have been the first caliph. They said only direct descendants of Muhammad should lead the Muslim community, and that Ali had been cheated of his

وَقَالَ يَا مُحَمَّدُ رَبُّكَ يَقْرَأُكَ السَّلَامَ وَيَخُصُّكَ بِالتَّحِيَّةِ وَالإِكْرَامِ

حَقُّ تَعَالَى سَكَا سَلَامٌ قَلْدِي اِبْتِدَى اِشْتَهْ جَبْرَائِيلِي

سَكَا كُونْدِرْدُوم كَه سَنُوكْ أَمْرُوكَه مُطِيعُ اُولَاسِنُكْ

دُوشْمَنْلَرْ وَكِي هَلَاكْ اِيْلِيَه بِنْ نِكَه كُو كَاوِكْ دِبْلَرْ

right. In this contentious situation, some disaffected members of the army led an uprising and killed Uthman in 656.

The elders of the community then chose Ali as the fourth caliph. But some Muslims revolted against him, saying he wasn't acting fast enough against Uthman's killers. At the same time, the governor of Syria, Muawiyah ibn Abi Sufyan (602–680), challenged Ali for the caliphate. Unrest grew and finally Ali's army faced Muawiyah's in the Battle at Siffin. The battle was inconclusive and both parties agreed to arbitration, but a section of Ali's supporters withdrew, saying a divine right couldn't be put to human judgment. This group, known as the Khwarij, murdered Ali in 661. Muawiyah wrested control of the caliphate.

At this point, a majority of Muslims agreed to Muawiyah's rule, preferring security to mayhem. These Muslims became known as Sunnis, believing that any leader who agreed to follow Muhammad's example was a legitimate leader. Other Muslims, who believed that only descendants of the Prophet should rule, championed the cause of Ali's sons, Hasan and Hussein. They came to be

This sixteenth-century manuscript page by Mustafa Parir is from *Siyar-I Nabi (Life of the Prophet)*. Although conservative Muslims frown upon rendering the human form in religious texts, this leaf depicts a veiled Muhammad, Abu Bakr al-Asamm, and Ali ibn Abi Talib traveling to Mecca. This manuscript was commissioned in 1594 by the Ottoman sultan Murad III and is said to be written by a blind Turkish poet.

known as Shia Muslims (or Shiites), and from then on they had their own line of religious leaders, called imams.

Muawiyah shifted the capital to Damascus from Medina, and his dynastic successors are known as the Umayyads. After a few turbulent decades, an era of relative peace came with the rule of Abd al-Malik (646–705). He had the Dome of the Rock built in Jerusalem, one of the first grand monuments in the distinct Muslim architectural style. He also established a uniform currency, expanded the postal system, and made Arabic the official language across the empire.

The capital in Damascus was closer to the Mediterranean and North Africa, leading to a fruitful cultural interaction. Muslims came into contact with Christian sects. In the east, they adopted the administrative structure of the Sassanid dynasty, and many newly converted Sassanid functionaries began working for the Muslim governors.

Taxes and tributes strengthened the government. At the same time, expanding trade brought many Muslims untold wealth. They maintained luxurious lifestyles, opulent homes, and beautiful mosques. Many of them took to patronizing the arts and sciences, commissioning both artistic and philosophic endeavors. In the early period there was an emphasis on religious studies as scholars studied the Qur'an. This extensive study and interpretation was linked to the development of Islamic law, which involved extrapolation from the Qur'an and Muhammad's sayings and actions. Literature

The oldest surviving mosque, the Umayyad Mosque of Damascus, is rendered in this detail from a seventeenth-century painting. Commissioned during the reign of Umayyad caliph Abd al-Malik between 705 and 715, it is considered the first great work of Muslim architecture. Built upon the Roman Temple of Jupiter and later that of a Christian church, the site was long considered holy. Upon deciding to create a great mosque there in 705, the caliph exclaimed, "Inhabitants of Damascus, four things give you marked superiority over the rest of the world: your climate, your water, your fruits, and your baths. To these I wanted to add a fifth: this mosque."

also bloomed since the Arabian Peninsula and the Middle East had a rich literary history of pre-Muslim scholars who worked to systematize the Arabic language.

THE ABBASIDS

In AD 750, a group who claimed direct descent from Abbas, the Prophet's uncle, overthrew the Umayyad dynasty. The group founded the Abbasid dynasty and soon moved the seat of power from Damascus to Baghdad.

Because the Baghdad region had been controlled by the Sassanid dynasty, the Abbasid leaders adopted its system of government. Soon, Persians came to hold high posts in the caliphate. Unlike the Umayyads who saw Islam as an Arab religion, the Abbasids stressed that Arabs and converts to Islam from other groups were equals.

The Abbasid caliphs found themselves in a stronger economic position than their predecessors. They had more time and resources to promote religious, cultural, and educational pursuits and had a better means of defense.

By this time, Muslims had embraced Greek learning, which though shunned in Europe by the Catholic Church, was flourishing in Alexandria, Egypt. The Nestorians, a Christian sect who spoke Syriac, had fled the Byzantine Empire and moved into Muslim lands, bringing with them copies of Greek texts on philosophy and natural sciences.

In Persia, the Sassanids had established a school at Jundishapur, where they gathered Indian, Christian, and Jewish scholars. This school helped assimilate Indian mathematics, astronomy, and astrology with Greco-Roman traditions.

Most Muslims were eager to partake in this sharing of knowledge. A famous saying attributed to the prophet Muhammad exhorts all believers to seek knowledge, even if it means traveling to China—which was then on the edge of the known world for Muslims.

But some Muslims didn't think it was wise to adopt foreign learning; they were especially wary of applying Greek philosophical methods to Islamic thought. But one of the first great philosopher-scientists of Islam, Yaqub ibn Ishaq al-Sabah al-Kindi (?–870), wrote in the ninth century in his work known as the *Rasa 'il al-Kindi*,

> We should not be ashamed to acknowledge truth and to assimilate it from whatever source it comes to us, even if it is brought to us from former generations and foreign peoples. For him who seeks the truth there is nothing of higher value than truth itself; it never cheapens or abases him who reaches for it, but ennobles and honors.

The victorious Muslim armies brought back more than books. When they conquered central Asia in AD 751, they took more than 20,000 Chinese prisoners to Samarqand. The Chinese knew how to make paper and gunpowder, and

Abbasid caliph Harun al-Rashid is depicted in this seventeenth-century Indian miniature painting. Remembered more for his patronage of the arts than his leadership skills, al-Rashid was a Persian scholar and a poet who loved storytelling. Al-Rashid's reign was one marked by increased trade and prosperity and was memorialized in the story *One Thousand and One Nights*.

soon these technologies began to spread. The availability of paper helped speed up translation and writing in the Muslim world and beyond it.

The fourth Abbasid caliph, Harun al-Rashid (766–809), began ruling in AD 786. He started a library that housed works from across the empire. Al-Rashid also commissioned translations. He promoted Arabic literature, and scholars started compiling the tales of the famous *One Thousand and One Nights*, or *Arabian Nights* as it is more commonly known. He established diplomatic contacts with European rulers and sent King Charlemagne (742–814) an elephant and a water clock, both then unknown in Europe.

This period is sometimes called the golden age of Islam, when Baghdad was the center of culture and learning. Scholars and artists from across the known world traveled to the city to avail themselves of the support the caliphs showered on the arts and sciences.

Harun al-Rashid's son al-Mamun (813–833) inherited his father's love of knowledge. In 830, he established the Bayt al-Hikma (House of Wisdom), a library, translation center, academy, and observatory in Baghdad. Al-Mamun gathered multilingual scholars to translate Greek, Persian, and Sanskrit texts and welcomed learned men. Muhammad ibn Musa al-Khwarizmi (780–850), the father of algebra (which got its name from the title of his book, *Kitab al-Jabr*), worked at the House of Wisdom. Another celebrated scholar was a

Hunayn and the House of Wisdom

One of the Bayt al-Hikma's most important and prolific contributors was Hunayn ibn Ishaq al-Ibadi, a Nestorian Christian known in the West as Johannitius. Al-Ibadi was probably from southern Persia. His native language was Syriac, but he was also fluent in Greek and Arabic, and he began translating texts at the age of seventeen. Al-Ibadi was a physician by education and he translated nearly all the Greek medical texts available at the time, including ninety-five Syriac and thirty-four Arabic versions of works by Galen.

Al-Ibadi was the lead translator at the Bayt al-Hikma and also served as chief physician to the caliph al-Mutawakkil. He wrote several original medical treatises as well as commentaries on the texts he translated.

As one of the pioneers in the translation movement, al-Ibadi was confronted with the difficult task of translating complex concepts from Greek to Arabic. Later scholars remarked that he achieved a great degree of accuracy and sensitivity in his translations, and helped establish new Arabic terms for philosophical, medical, and scientific concepts. His son Ishaq ibn Hunayn, who was equally gifted, followed in his footsteps.

Unfortunately, ibn Ishaq al-Ibadi's church was not pleased with some of al-Ibadi's work and he was excommunicated. A deeply religious man, al-Ibadi was apparently devastated and committed suicide at the age of sixty-six.

Nestorian Christian, Hunayn ibn Ishaq al-Ibadi (808–873), who published many original works and commentaries. A little later, around 900–950, Al-Azhar University in Cairo, and Damascus University in Syria were established, two centuries before the first university in Europe.

THE SCIENCES

Muslims were also making great strides in the sciences. It was at the House of Wisdom that Greek geometry met Indian arithmetic, resulting in the system of Arabic numerals (Arabs called them Hindi numbers) and the concept of zero, replacing the cumbersome Roman numerals. As already noted, al-Khwarizmi developed algebra, including linear and quadratic equations, and applied it to contracts, land surveys, and tax collection. He also developed algorithms; this term is also derived from his name.

Other mathematicians delved into binomials and polynomials. Concepts in geometry originally introduced by Euclid and Archimedes were further developed, laying the groundwork for the modern system that emerged centuries later. Muslims made advances in trigonometry, discovering the cosine, and developing the remaining trigonometric functions: sine, tangent, cotangent, secant, and cosecant. The needs of a growing empire and thriving trade also led to the innovation of double entry, a method of bookkeeping that is still used across the world.

Muslims were especially attracted to medical sciences. The Qur'an says God has a cure for every disease, and physicians were eager to find those cures. The Abbasids promoted medical learning, and hospitals were established with permanent endowments. The first was built in the 800s in Baghdad under Harun al-Rashid. Within 100 years, there were five other hospitals, or *bimaristans*, in Baghdad alone. In addition to general physicians, hospitals had ophthalmologists, surgeons, and bonesetters on staff. The government even sent doctors with traveling pharmacies to care for prisoners on a daily basis.

In applied chemistry, Muslims discovered better and more efficient ways for tanning leather and forging metals. They developed many compounds and substances, some medicinal. The names of many substances, such as alcohol, camphor, borax, and elixir, are derived from Arabic names.

Muslims also focused on astronomy, as it was important to determine the positions of heavenly bodies to know in which direction to pray toward Mecca. Muslims were also interested in maritime sciences since they used to sail to Africa, India, and Southeast Asia to trade. They tried to correct and refine Ptolemy's (100–170) *Almagest*. Muslims used the mariners' compass and made improvements to the existing design of the astrolabe and typical nautical maps. Muslim astronomers knew Earth was round and successfully calculated its circumference. It is possible that Abu al-Hasan al-Ashari (873–936) invented the basic tubular telescope,

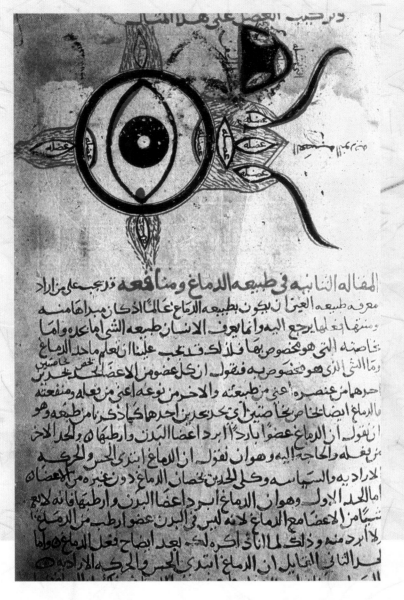

This diagram of the eye is from *Kitab al-Ashr Maqalat fi' l Ayn* (*Book of the Ten Treatises on the Eye*), a work that presented the first anatomical drawings of the human eye. The manuscript was written by Hunayn ibn Ishaq al-Ibadi. A Nestorian Christian probably better known in the West as a translator of ancient Greek texts by Galen and Hippocrates, al-Ibadi was also a qualified physician and pharmacist. Educated in Baghdad and an expert linguist, he was widely traveled and his original and translated texts on the structure, diseases, and treatments of the eye formed the basis for the field of ophthalmology.

though some historians also note that the instrument may have been in use earlier by the ancient Greeks. Muslim scientists invented the pendulum and also pioneered the use of hydraulic presses and water clocks, which tracked the passage of time and the phases of the moon.

Abu Ali al-Hasan ibn al-Haytham (Alhazan) (965–1039) developed a theory of vision. In his *Book of Optics*, he takes a mathematical approach to understanding sight, reflection, and the refraction of light and color. He also developed some of the principles on which the modern camera works. Al-Haytham was the first to understand that the eye perceives images because of light rays reflected off the object.

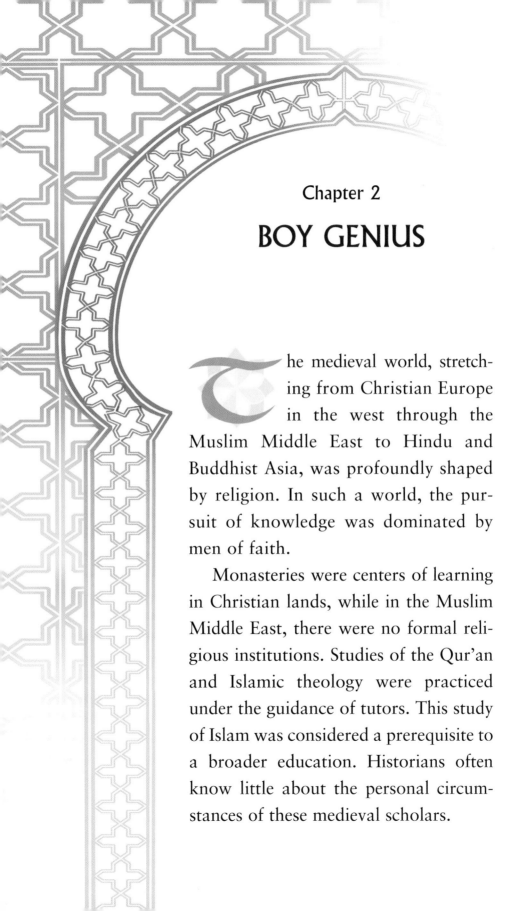

Chapter 2

BOY GENIUS

The medieval world, stretching from Christian Europe in the west through the Muslim Middle East to Hindu and Buddhist Asia, was profoundly shaped by religion. In such a world, the pursuit of knowledge was dominated by men of faith.

Monasteries were centers of learning in Christian lands, while in the Muslim Middle East, there were no formal religious institutions. Studies of the Qur'an and Islamic theology were practiced under the guidance of tutors. This study of Islam was considered a prerequisite to a broader education. Historians often know little about the personal circumstances of these medieval scholars.

In the case of Avicenna, we have access to some information about his early years in the form of a brief autobiographical sketch he dictated to his student Abu Ubayid al-Juzjani. It covers approximately the first thirty years of his life, up to the point he met al-Juzjani, who became his lifelong disciple and companion, and who later wrote an account of the rest of his master's life.

Avicenna was born into a Persian family in the village of Afshana, near Bukhara, in 980. His mother's name was Sitara, and his father, Abd Allah, a native of Balkh, was the governor of Kharmaithan, near Bukhara. After the birth of Avicenna's younger brother five years later, their father moved the family to Bukhara, so his sons would have greater opportunities. At the time, Bukhara was the administrative capital of the Samanid caliphate, the court under which Avicenna eventually worked.

THE SAMANIDS

Central Asia had been under Muslim rule for nearly 100 years by the time Avicenna was born. The local rulers had generally accepted the supremacy of the caliphate in Baghdad but sometimes fought battles with each other.

This tower is part of the Kalan Mosque located in Bukhara, Uzbekistan, Avicenna's birth city. It was and is still common for Muslims to build tall minarets, parapets from which they call other faithful Muslims for their daily prayers. Bukhara is the oldest city in Uzbekistan, and this tower and mosque complex was built in 1127.

The founder of the Samanid dynasty was Saman-Khoda (also known as Khudat), a Persian convert to Islam who challenged the Tahirid rulers who had been battling Baghdad for dominance. Caliph al-Mamun rewarded Saman-Khoda's grandsons with the governorships of Samarqand, Fergana, Shash (all in present-day Uzbekistan), and Herat (in present-day Afghanistan).

One of Saman-Khoda's great-grandsons, Esmail, who ruled as caliph from 892 to 907, defeated the Tahirids and established himself in Bukhara. In so doing, he won the recognition of Caliph al-Mutadid, though he did not pay the yearly tribute expected of other vassal states.

By the ninth century, Bukhara had grown into an urban center from a group of villages clustered around an oasis on the Zarafshan River. It was a fertile region renowned for its fruit, including pomegranates, apricots, and cherries, and was a vibrant stop on the trade routes running from the Byzantine cities of Rome and Constantinople, through the Middle East, and on to China and even Russia.

The Samanids were Sunni Muslims who were tolerant of other Muslim sects, including Shiites, and people of other religions. They were Persian descendants and revived aspects of the Persian Sassanid dynasty.

In an attempt to re-create the glories of ancient Persia, the Samanids reinstated Persian as the state language—written in Arabic script—and ushered in a cultural revival.

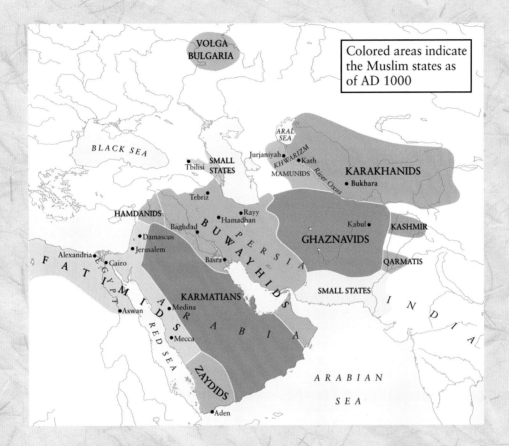

Colored areas indicate the Muslim states as of AD 1000

Although central Asia was under Samanid control from about AD 819 to 999, the Turkic Karakhanids overthrew Samanid caliphs in 999, eliminating the last major Persian dynasty. This map shows prevailing Muslim states in AD 1000, just after the Samanid collapse. Samanid caliphs ruled for less than 200 years, but they provided enough political and social stability in the region to support a rise in culture, education, and religious tolerance; a revival of the Persian language and beautiful architecture; and the establishment of a currency system. Bukhara, the birthplace of Avicenna, was among the capitals of the Samanid dynasty.

They supported Arab and Persian poets, writers, and philosophers, and they collected books. The Samanids also sent emissaries to different kingdoms to meet intellectuals, encouraging them to make Bukhara their home. Samanid sultans commissioned scholarly works, including commentaries on the Qur'an, medical discoveries, astronomy, and geography.

By the time Avicenna was born in 980, the Samanids' grip was loosening on the outlying areas of their territory. They were soon powerless to stop revolts by local administrators. As time passed, the political climate in the region became more turbulent, as Avicenna would witness in his lifetime.

EARLY EDUCATION

Avicenna's father was a member of the ruling elite, and he was eager that his son be given the best education possible. At that time, the finest education meant learning Arabic in order to read the Qur'an. The next steps in his education were the *hadith*, learning the sayings of Muhammad as recorded and passed down by his companions; followed by learning Islamic law (*sharia*); and jurisprudence (*fiqh*). He also studied grammar, poetry, and literature.

In his dictated memoir, known together with al-Juzjani's account as *Life of Ibn Sina (Sarguzisht-i-Ibn Sina)*, Avicenna says, "I was put under teachers of the Qur'an and letters. By

A Muslim teacher is seen with his students in this thirteenth-century Turkish miniature by al-Monbacchir called *The Philosopher*. Muslim students who studied medicine were also taught in similarly sized groups. They were offered courses in music, mathematics, astronomy, philosophy, and geometry. Students hoping to become physicians one day continued their education by learning medical theory. They received clinical instruction and observed surgery in much the same way as today's educational hospitals.

the time I was ten, I had mastered the Qur'an and a great deal of literature, so that I was marveled for my aptitude."

That Avicenna had mastered the Qur'an by memorizing it at such an early age is evidence of his amazing memory, an ability that would prove especially useful in later years when he was almost constantly on the road, moving from one town to another, without access to his books or manuscripts. During those times, Avicenna often wrote from memory.

Like their rulers, Avicenna's family was likely Sunni, though some later critics have said it was Shiite. Avicenna studied the Hanafi school of Sunni law with the learned scholar Ismail al-Zahid. This particular scholar's works shaped Hanafi, one of the four schools of thought in the Sunni branch of Islam. The other three Sunni schools of thought are Shafi, Hanbali, and Maliki, but Hanafi law, considered moderate, was predominant in Bukhara at the time.

During Avicenna's youth, his father knew of the importance of mathematical methods unique to south Asia, for Indians were already using the decimal system and the concept of zero. An Indian grocer was located who could teach young Avicenna the system.

Avicenna grew up amid philosophical and religious discussions and an atmosphere of constant learning. He mentions his exposure to Shiite Ismaili philosophy, when his father entertained missionaries of the sect, but says that even at a young age he remained unconvinced.

It was clear that Avicenna was a gifted child. After he completed his religious studies, his father hired a philosophy and science teacher, Abu Abd Allah al-Natali, as a resident tutor. With him, Avicenna started his study of the Greek philosophical works through Arabic translations. According to Avicenna's memoir, dictated to his companion al-Juzjani,

Avicenna began with a translation of the *Isagoge* by Porphyry (234–305), an introduction to Aristotle's *Organon*, the philosopher's collected works on logic and his theory of logic and syllogisms. According to al-Juzjani, Avicenna said in *Life of Ibn Sina*:

> [Al-Natali] was extremely amazed at me; whatever problem he posed I conceptualized better than he, so he advised my father against my taking up any occupation other than learning.

Through learning Sunni law, or *fiqh*, Avicenna had already been exposed to practical logic and deductive reasoning. Logic is the science that studies the principles and criteria of inference and demonstration, or the structure of arguments. Its aim is to distinguish between reasonable and poor arguments. Logic is often applied as a form of reasoning, consisting of a major premise, a minor premise, and a conclusion. For example, the statement "All humans are mortal" would be considered a major premise, while the statement "I am a human" would be considered a minor premise. Therefore, the conclusion to this argument is "I am mortal." This three-point structure is known as a syllogism, a form of deduction that philosophers use to express universal truths. In order to test the validity of any theory, a philosopher examines its logic. If the premises are faulty, the inference is faulty, creating a fallacy.

A categorical syllogism contains precisely three terms: the major term, which is the predicate of the conclusion; the minor term, the subject of the conclusion; and the middle term, which appears in both premises, but not in the conclusion. Thus one categorical syllogism could be: All philosophers are men (middle term); all men are mortal; therefore, all philosophers (minor term) are mortal (major term). Venn diagrams are a pictorial representation of categorical syllogisms. To make accurate syllogisms, it is necessary to classify everything in appropriate genera and subcategories. Thus, in the above argument, philosophers are categorized as humans. Humans can be a larger category of mammals, and so on.

The middle term is considered the key to a syllogism, and it is considered the key to moving an argument forward. According to Avicenna, mastering this logic marks men of learning and higher ability from others.

Studying Aristotle's *Organon*, Avicenna stunned al-Natali by taking an unconventional approach to the concept of genus, and on how to isolate the middle terms. As Avicenna recalled in his memoir, "Whatever problem he stated to me, I showed a better mental conception of it."

After logic, al-Natali introduced Avicenna to mathematics through the works of Euclid and Ptolemy, walking him through the first few theorems and leaving him to read the rest himself. "Such autonomy is the mark of truth," Avicenna later wrote in his memoir.

"Teaching provides only a hint of the problems, which the real intelligence solves for itself." This experience would color much of Avicenna's later philosophy. His book *The Living Son of the Vigilant* (*Hayy ibn Yaqzan*), chronicles how humans can reach the truth independently by describing how a child living alone on an island discovers God through nature. Avicenna's autobiography also emphasizes the importance of independent learning.

When al-Natali left Bukhara, Avicenna continued to read on his own. He

The Greco-Roman mathematician Euclid can be seen in this fifteenth-century painting. Euclid is best remembered for the *Elements,* his treatise on geometry, which was read and studied centuries later by Avicenna.

studied various works on the natural sciences and philosophy. He read Aristotle's *Metaphysica*, but it made little sense to him at thirteen. He recalled reading it forty times, until he had it memorized, but admitted that he still couldn't make out its true purpose. Still hungry for knowledge, Avicenna next turned to medicine.

This fifteenth-century copy of the French manuscript *Chirurgia Magna*, which was originally written in 1363 by Guy de Chauliac, features images of the physicians Galen, Hippocrates, and Avicenna. De Chauliac (1300–1367) was among the most famous of the European surgeons of the Middle Ages. *Chirurgia Magna* describes the use of inhalants as sleeping agents as well as a variety of surgical procedures. Along with Avicenna's *Canon*, it was a standard medical text in Europe for centuries.

AVICENNA THE PHYSICIAN

After he read works of philosophy and the sciences, Avicenna stated in his memoir, "Next, I desired to study medicine, and proceeded to read all the books that have been written on this subject."

Muslim medicine at that time was greatly influenced by Greek tradition. Avicenna pored over the translated works of both Hippocrates and Galen, who was physician to Marcus Aurelius. Galen's knowledge was adopted and improved upon by an array of scholarly physicians before Avicenna, including Yaqub ibn Ishaq al-Sabah al-Kindi; and the great Persian physician Abu Bakr Muhammad ibn Zakariya al-Razi (865–932).

Al-Razi's most famous work is the nine-volume *The Virtuous Life* (*Havi*), a medical encyclopedia in which he wrote about new discoveries. He was the first to use alcohol as an antiseptic and made fine strings from animal intestines for sewing wounds. Al-Razi was the first to write about the symptoms and treatment of smallpox and chicken pox.

Even though conflicts between Shiites and Sunnis continued, the Abbasids revered intellectualism and made time to expand libraries and centers of learning. They had established hospitals with teaching facilities where doctors practiced and taught. Al-Razi headed the Muqtedari Hospital in Baghdad that maintained a well-rounded curriculum, in line with the concept that a truly learned man had more than one area of expertise. Pharmacology, or the study and identification of medicines, was highly developed and most hospitals maintained herb gardens and pharmacies.

The precocious Avicenna, who could not have been more than fifteen years of age at this time, soon became a skilled physician. He stated in his autobiography, "Medicine is not a difficult science, and naturally I excelled in it at a very short time, so that qualified physicians began to read medicine with me."

Avicenna continued to practice medicine throughout his life. During good times he treated people for free. When he had no other means, he would make his livelihood from clinics he established, where he stated in his memoir, "the methods of treatment derived from practical experience revealed themselves to me such [ways that] . . . baffle description."

After studying medicine, Avicenna began rereading texts on philosophy and logic. During this time, he claimed that he had not been sleeping through the night. If he felt sleepy or weak, he would drink coffee to help him stay alert, or if he was trying to solve a particularly difficult problem, he would go to a mosque and pray until the answer came to him. But despite his ability as a philosopher, it was medicine that would open the next door in Avicenna's life.

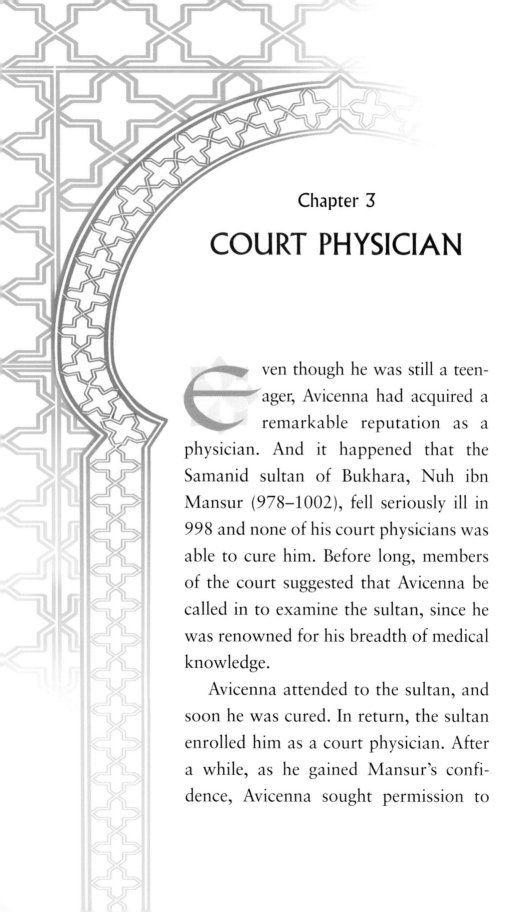

Chapter 3

COURT PHYSICIAN

Even though he was still a teen-ager, Avicenna had acquired a remarkable reputation as a physician. And it happened that the Samanid sultan of Bukhara, Nuh ibn Mansur (978–1002), fell seriously ill in 998 and none of his court physicians was able to cure him. Before long, members of the court suggested that Avicenna be called in to examine the sultan, since he was renowned for his breadth of medical knowledge.

Avicenna attended to the sultan, and soon he was cured. In return, the sultan enrolled him as a court physician. After a while, as he gained Mansur's confidence, Avicenna sought permission to

enter the royal library. The library's huge collection of books on all subjects, from literature to philosophy to astronomy, rivaled that of Baghdad. Avicenna described it as a mansion filled with many chambers, each one filled with books on a particular subject. For Avicenna, it was as if someone had handed him the keys to the world. He spent the next year devouring the contents of the library.

By the time Avicenna was eighteen, he had made his way through the library's storehouse of knowledge. "My memory for learning was at that period of my life better than it is now," he stated in his autobiography, "but today I am more mature; apart from this my knowledge is exactly the same, nothing further having been added to my store since then."

The following year, the library was destroyed in a fire, and Avicenna's detractors—he already had many—accused him of setting the blaze, "so that he could attribute the contents of those books to himself," according to one of Avicenna's modern biographers, S. M. Afnan. Avicenna, a Persian with a father who had dabbled with Shiite doctrine, was an easy target.

This watercolor of a group of Persian court physicians is from the *Shahnameh* (*Book of Kings*), an epic poem of 60,000 couplets by the greatest Persian poet, Ferdowsi (935–1020), a contemporary of Avicenna's. Completed in 1010, the *Book of Kings* was a sweeping history of Persian royalty to the year 628. It took thirty-five years to write and was first presented by Ferdowsi to Mahmud of Ghazna, a sultan who sought Avicenna for his court around 1000.

Shortly after, at the request of a neighbor, Avicenna wrote the *Kitab al-Majmu*, or *The Compendium*, a book that covered all branches of knowledge except math. He was twenty-one, and soon after he was commissioned for two other works by a lawyer—one a commentary on legal matters called *Book of Import and Substance* (*Kitab al-Hasil w'al-Mahsul*) and another was a work on ethics called *Book of Good Work and Evil* (*Kitab al-Birr w'al-lthm*).

As previously noted, Avicenna was interested in metaphysics, having read Aristotle's *Metaphysica*, but was unable to understand it fully. Aristotle's ideas, however, had became clearer to Avicenna shortly before he came into the service of Sultan Nuh ibn Mansur. He was on a booksellers' street when a vendor approached him with a copy of Abu Nasr al-Farabi's (878–950) commentary on *Metaphysica*. Avicenna admits that at first he wasn't interested, because of his futile experience with the original work, but the seller was persuasive and offered it at a great discount. Avicenna says he rushed home to read it, and it was as if all of Aristotle's intentions were revealed to him. In gratitude, he says, he went out the next day to give charity to the poor.

UNDERSTANDING METAPHYSICS

Following the Aristotelian system, Avicenna believed that philosophy encompassed the pursuit of all knowledge.

Philosophy can be divided into practical applications such as economics, politics, and ethics; and the more speculative pursuits, that included theology, mathematics, and physics. All six sciences have pure and applied aspects. Avicenna regarded theology as the most important of sciences because it involves the study of God and creation and unites all of the branches of learning, since everything leads back to the creator. In keeping with this philosophy, knowledge is the criterion by which souls will be judged in the afterlife.

Avicenna learned that Aristotle believed that the principle governing the world was motion. Things were constantly in a state of change. Since everything in the universe is in motion, Aristotle regarded the universe as eternal. But there must be something that put the universe in motion. According to Aristotle, this prime mover was God. Plato, on the other hand, conceived of God as pure good or pure intellect. In Plato's opinion, God didn't create, but rather emanated the universe, like the sun emits light. Plato thought that the objects in this world were imperfect copies of permanent forms that existed in an "intelligible" world.

Independent of the Greeks, Muslim theologians had built a collection of writings and opinions about God and creation that were derived from the Qur'an. They considered the Qur'an a miraculous revelation and proof of the existence of

In this miniature from a sixteenth-century copy of the Persian manuscript *Khamseh* (*The Quintuplet*), the Greek philosopher Plato is seen charming wild animals with his music. *Khamseh* was a series of five epic poems in 30,000 rhymed couplets written by the romantic Persian poet Elyas Yusof Nezami Ganjavi (1141–1209). Persians were known for writing historical narratives in the form of poetic verse. Avicenna was also fond of documenting life in rhyming couplets.

God. They debated questions about God and his attributes, fate, free will, and the afterlife. They examined whether the world was eternal or created, and whether God controlled every individual occurrence in the universe. When faced with Greek rationalism, many theologians adopted a methodological argument to secure their position, which is often called the *kalam* school of thought.

Scholars in this tradition were called *mutakallimun* (those who practice kalam, or discussion and debate), and their argument, to put it simply, was that it is clear that the world exists. And since the world exists, there must be something that caused it to exist, and that something is God. They recognized that this argument could be used to ask who made God, but they argued that this would create an infinite chain, which would be absurd. Instead, they said the chain stopped with God, who created the universe from nothing and controlled every aspect of it, from the stars, to a falling leaf, to every human action. Thus, the mutakallimum rejected the notion of natural laws and the rational concept of cause and effect, since they believed that God caused everything.

But many Muslim scholars were taken by the Aristotelian emphasis on rationality and reason and the Neoplatonic school of thought derived from Plato.

The most important of these was Abu Nasr al-Farabi, who is regarded as one of the greatest of Muslim philosophers,

This portrait of the Muslim philosopher Abu Nasr al-Farabi (878–950) was taken from a contemporary bank note from Kazakhstan. Al-Farabi was known to adapt ancient Greek philosophical ideas to Muslim faith and ideology.

and among all thinkers, second only to Aristotle. Al-Farabi disagreed with the mutakallimun and instead developed a concept of emanation. He argued that God is the First Being, from whom emerges the First Intellect. That First Intellect reflects on itself, and in doing so, produces the First Heaven and the Second Intellect. This process continues until the Tenth Intellect, which produces the moon and Earth. It was al-Farabi's work that helped unlock the full meaning of Aristotle's metaphysics for Avicenna.

AVICENNA'S DOCTRINES

Avicenna dealt with metaphysics in several of his later works, most comprehensively in his *Book of Healing* (*Kitab* al-Shifa), which was a compendium on several subjects that he wrote over twelve years.

In the sections on God, existence, and the human soul, Avicenna sought to reconcile his belief in God, whom the Qur'an describes as the creator of the world, with the rationalism and logical method he learned from the Greeks.

Avicenna begins the *Book of Healing* by stating, "There is no doubt that there is existence"—this is something humans know immediately, as a form of self-consciousness. Then he makes a distinction between forms of existence, arguing that we can imagine that nothing in this world exists. But if we try to imagine there is no cause for the world, we are unable to do so, since we know that the world exists and there has to be something that caused it to exist. This something is God. Avicenna calls God the Necessary Being, since we cannot logically imagine a world without him. Everything else is merely "possible." That is, it need not have existed, but it does because God caused it to, and in that sense it is necessarily existent.

But this argument relied on man's intuitive abilities, and Avicenna also proposed to rationally prove God's existence and the universe. To do this, he presented a unique and important philosophical distinction between essence and existence.

Essence, for Avicenna, was the defining characteristics of a thing—living or inanimate. For example, "human-ness" encompasses the characteristics that make a mammal a human. He distinguished this essence from existence, which is the addition of matter to an essence. Therefore, all humans may not be alike, though they share the same essence. Avicenna also noted that it is possible to conceive of an essence without it having an existence, because an essence itself cannot cause it. But there is one being whose essence cannot be contemplated without its actual existence, and that is God, because in him, essence and existence are the same.

Avicenna weaved this notion of God as the Necessary Being with al-Farabi's system of emanation, but for Avicenna, the intellects are the archangels and the tenth (intellect) is the Active Intellect that gave rise to our earthly world, emanating souls and giving them form. These heav-enly beings may cause things, but they cannot create something from nothing, as God can; they need matter on which to act. Avicenna also argued that although God caused the universe, it was eternal, emanating from God's self-knowledge, and was caused because it is an aspect of his essence.

This metaphysical structure allowed Avicenna to regard God as the creator, but a very remote creator—the being who

In this print, Avicenna is seen surrounded by his students, whom he taught whenever possible. Avicenna himself had an unquenchable thirst for knowledge. In the biography about Avicenna, al-Juzjani writes, "During the 25 years I accompanied and served him I never saw him to take a new book and read it right through; he looked always for the difficult passages and complicated problems and examined what the author had said on these, so as to discover what his degree of learning and level of understanding might be."

The Floating Man

In his discussions of existence, and specifically the existence of a soul and consciousness, Avicenna put forth a unique idea. In *Kitab al-Shifa*'s section on psychology, he said:

> *Imagine a man created all at once and in perfect bodily condition, but whose eyes are screened so as to prevent him from perceiving external things. Imagine further that this man floats in empty air [vacuum] in such a manner that he has no sensation, not even such as may be caused by the touch and friction of air.*

Such a man, Avicenna argued, will still be able to reflect upon himself and affirm his own existence, though he won't be able to prove he has a body, or that anything other than his self-consciousness exists.

This concept is considered revolutionary because it foreshadowed one of the most important doctrines of the eighteenth-century period of Enlightenment, René Descartes' famous three words, *Cogito, ergo sum*—"I think, therefore I am." Descartes arrived at this conclusion because he rejected tradition and cast doubts upon everything. But to doubt one's own existence required thought, which in turn proves one's existence. This philosophy asserted humans as rational beings, giving prominence to the idea of mind over matter, or even the soul.

started the universe, but does not intervene in its functioning. Thus, Avicenna incorporated scientific principles and the rational concept of cause and effect with his religious beliefs. In keeping with this philosophy, although God is the ultimate creator of humankind, he does not predetermine the course of human life the way most Muslim scholars believed. Humans exercise free will within the boundaries of the laws of nature.

Frans Hals painted this portrait of the seventeenth-century philosopher René Descartes. Like Avicenna had centuries earlier, Descartes developed specific theories about the creation of the world, God, and human beings.

One modern scholar, Professor J. L. Teichel of Cambridge University, described Avicenna's argument as a "creative evolution." Every new development is a possibility, but it occurs within limits set by the prior process of evolution.

Avicenna believed that through logic and reasoning, humans can grasp the underlying framework that governs this world and the being that led to its creation; thus, humans can achieve knowledge of God. In fact, to

Avicenna, understanding God was the ultimate realization of human potential and spirituality.

MOVING ON

When Avicenna was twenty-two years old, his father died. In his autobiography, Avicenna said that he took an administrative post under the Samanid rulers, but around 999, he moved to Gurganj in Khiva (present-day Turkmenistan). It is possible that the same religious and racial tensions that had surfaced during the burning of the library may have forced him to leave Bukhara.

Turkish power was on the rise as could be witnessed with the growing influence of Sultan Mahmud of Ghazna (971–1030). Mahmud later sought Avicenna for his court, but the scholar avoided him, fearing his capricious and violent temperament. Someone had even accused Avicenna being a blasphemer, because he believed the world was eternal and he denied that humans would be resurrected physically on the day of judgment.

Avicenna also denied that humans could define God. In Muslim tradition and in the Qur'an, God is known by various names including, Most Merciful, All-Knowing, and All-Powerful, but Avicenna believed that the names could not be taken literally, drawing the wrath of most traditionalists.

In this watercolor from the *Shah-nameh* (*Book of Kings*), its author-poet, Ferdowsi, greets the poets in the court of the Sultan Mahmud of Ghazna. Avicenna met the sultan around 1000 when he was asked to join his court as a physician, though he declined, fearing the sultan's manic temperament. Avicenna, who sometimes wrote in couplets as eleventh-century Persian poets commonly did, could very well have made Ferdowsi's acquaintance as well.

Still, the vizier of Gurganj, a learned man, was pleased to host Avicenna. He introduced him to the emir, Ali ibn Mamun, who gave him a position at his court with a handsome salary. It was in Gurganj that Avicenna met another great philosopher-scientist, Abu Raihan al-Biruni (973–1048). But Avicenna's stay in Gurganj was short-lived. Avicenna was forced to flee again, this time for reasons unknown, though historians have noted that Sultan Mahmud of Ghazna was infuriated by Avicenna's refusal to join his court. He ordered the emir to deliver Avicenna and several other courtiers, including al-Biruni, to Ghazna.

The emir let the scholars know of the sultan's intentions, giving them the choice of going with the sultan's men, or escaping. Al-Biruni reluctantly chose to go to Ghazna, fearing Mahmud's wrath, but Avicenna and a Christian scholar, Abu Sahl al-Masihi, decided to flee since they had heard of Mahmud's intolerance and traditional beliefs.

Mahmud was infuriated and sent men to hunt them down; in fact, wanted posters were made featuring a portrait of Avicenna and distributed in the region. On the fourth day of his escape, he and al-Masihi got stuck in a sandstorm and his friend, unable to bear the heat, died of thirst.

Somehow Avicenna survived and eluded his hunters, traveling from town to town with the goal of reaching Jurjan (present-day Goran, Iran, at the southeastern end of the Caspian Sea). He wanted to enter the service of

Gunbad-i-Qabus, an emir noted for his love of learning. But by the time he got to Jurjan, Gunbad-i-Qabus had been overthrown and was in prison, where he was starved to death. Avicenna kept traveling, but he eventually returned to Jurjan where he met his lifelong friend Abu Ubayd al-Juzjani.

Avicenna soon found himself in a vexing situation. Because he had become so famous because of his knowledge, at least one leader was willing to have him kidnapped. Yet others were unwilling to hire him for fear of angering Mahmud. Upon considering his predicament, he composed the following couplet, which he mentions in his autobiography:

And great once I became, no more would Egypt have me,
And when my value rose, no one would care to buy me.

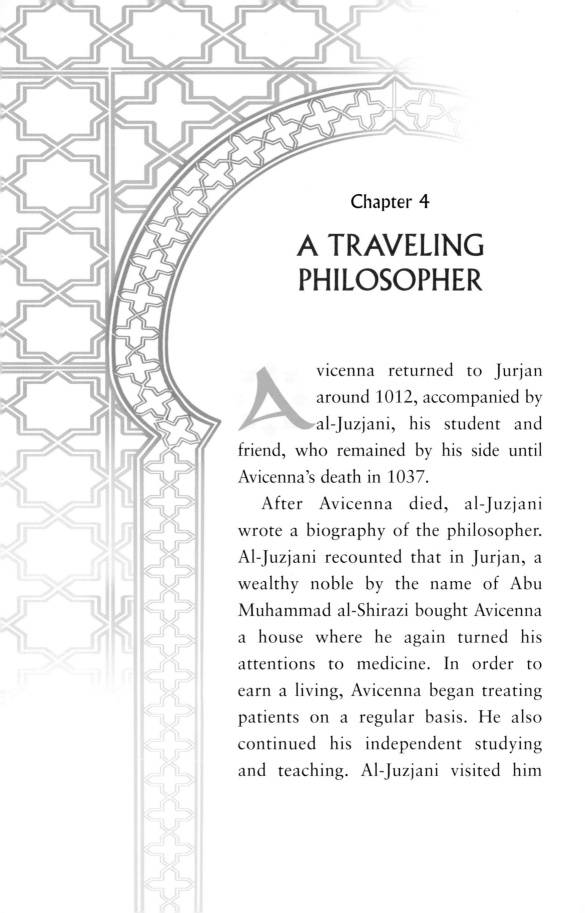

Chapter 4

A TRAVELING PHILOSOPHER

Avicenna returned to Jurjan around 1012, accompanied by al-Juzjani, his student and friend, who remained by his side until Avicenna's death in 1037.

After Avicenna died, al-Juzjani wrote a biography of the philosopher. Al-Juzjani recounted that in Jurjan, a wealthy noble by the name of Abu Muhammad al-Shirazi bought Avicenna a house where he again turned his attentions to medicine. In order to earn a living, Avicenna began treating patients on a regular basis. He also continued his independent studying and teaching. Al-Juzjani visited him

In this seventeenth-century illustration, court servants look on as a Muslim physician takes the pulse of a female patient in a garden filled with medicinal plants. At the same time, servants busy themselves by preparing medicines from the plants. The illustration was featured on the cover of a 1632 copy of Avicenna's *Canon of Medicine*. Muslims established the first pharmacies in the eighth century, and the fifth volume of the *Canon* was devoted to the preparation of more than 750 drugs.

every day, to hear his lectures on logic and to read Ptolemy's *Almagest*.

It was here that Avicenna, on the constant urging of al-Juzjani, began writing the *Canon*, the medical encyclopedia that would seal his fame as the "prince of physicians."

Soon after, Avicenna moved to the small principality of Rayy (near present-day Tehran, Iran). The ruler of Rayy was Majid al-Dawla, but in reality, the power behind the throne was his mother, al-Saiyyida, or "the Lady." She had assumed power on her husband's death because al-Dawla was a minor. Even when he came of age, she refused to hand over the throne.

Avicenna established a successful clinic and also offered his services at the royal court, where he was quickly welcomed. Al-Dawla was suffering from depression, probably because of his lack of influence, and Avicenna succeeded in alleviating his condition.

After two or three years, al-Dawla's own brother, Shams al-Dawla, ruler of Hamadan, attacked the city over the killing of an official.

By this time, Avicenna had managed to anger al-Saiyyida by giving his honest opinion that she should hand over power to her son, who was the legitimate heir. Unwelcome in Rayy, Avicenna again chose to flee.

THE *CANON OF MEDICINE*

The *Canon of Medicine*, a book of more than a million words in five volumes is Avicenna's masterpiece. In the opening to the first volume, he wrote:

> Medicine is a science from which one learns the status of the human body with respect to what is healthy and what is not, in order to preserve good health when it exists and restore it when it is lacking.

Book one of the *Canon* deals with the basic principles of medicine, drawing heavily on the early Greek traditions. It discusses the four elements—earth, water, air, and fire; and the four bodily fluids—yellow bile, black bile, blood, and phlegm. The latter were the four humors that were believed to govern a person's temperament. It was thought that good health depended on maintaining a balance between these humors. In addition, every substance was believed to have either a hot or cold property. Because it was believed that diseases caused an imbalance in these humors, physicians had to identify the imbalances and offer medicine, food, and care that would restore the patient's harmony.

Book one of the *Canon* also includes information related to human anatomy and the causes, symptoms, and treatments of diseases. Avicenna also discusses preventive measures and

emphasized the importance of good hygiene in the *Canon*, and wrote, "As long as the air is good and clean and not mixed by anything which is incompatible with the patient's temperament, health will materialize."

The second volume of the *Canon* lists the names of more than 700 medicinal plants and substances and for many centuries was the most comprehensive source of medicinal substances available. The third volume examines in detail diseases that affect particular parts of the body. The fourth volume explains various symptoms and diseases that affect the body as a whole, such as fevers, poisoning, and rashes, as well as wounds and fractures. Avicenna again returned to the importance of hygiene, emphasizing the need to take care of hair, skin, nails, and prevent body odor. It is in this section that he discusses problems and solutions for underweight and overweight people.

Avicenna also discusses psychological and emotional factors that affect health, and related illnesses such as

This illustration from Avicenna's *Canon of Medicine* includes information about the muscular system. Unprecedented in its sheer volume of information, the *Canon* became the authoritative source of medical information in the Muslim territories. Later, when European translations were made available in Latin, medical students the world over considered Avicenna's clinical observations as well as his comments on Greco-Roman medicine. In his prologue to the *Canterbury Tales*, the fourteenth-century English poet Geoffrey Chaucer (ca. 1342–1400) reminds readers that no doctor should be ignorant of Avicenna.

depression. He spoke of lovesickness, for which he prescribed uniting the pining person with his or her desire. He also believed that music could have a positive effect on persons of compromised health.

Volume five discusses how to mix substances to make medicines, and in what doses to administer them. Avicenna believed in experimentation. He offered seven rules for testing drugs, and advised testing them on animals to determine their effects. Avicenna's seven rules remain remarkably close to today's modern drug trials.

Avicenna combined his book learning with his clinical experience in order to write the *Canon*. And even though most of his clinical notes were lost by the time he sat down to compose the encyclopedia, he was able to rely on his legendary memory for extremely accurate descriptions.

Although Avicenna generally remained influenced by Greek medicine, he wasn't afraid to challenge its premises, as he did when he explained that a person could die from excessive blood to the head—such as from brain hemorrhages and tumors—which the ancients thought impossible. He was the first physician to say that tuberculosis was contagious, and centuries later he was proved correct.

Avicenna was also the first physician to recognize that germs can be transmitted through air, water, or soil, noting in the *Canon* "at certain times the air becomes infected and anyone breathing the infected air falls sick." He even said that the

Earthenware jugs such as these found in Rayy, Iran, were often used to hold and transport drug preparations during and after Avicenna's lifetime. Muslim pharmacies, which first appeared in Baghdad hospitals during the eighth century, became independent soon after. In Arabic, a pharmacist was called *as-saydanani* or *as-saydalani*, which means, "he who sells sandalwood." Muslims imported sandalwood from India and frequently used it in various drug preparations. At the same time, Muslims themselves contributed a variety of items to medical preparations including anise, cinnamon, cloves, camphor, and myrrh.

cause was tiny organisms that travel through air or water, a fact only verified centuries later through the invention of microscopes and the germ theory of disease. He correctly wrote that ancylostomiasis (hookworm infection) was caused by intestinal worms.

Avicenna on Cancer

Avicenna believed that cancers were caused by an excess of black bile, which caused excessive heat in the body. Like the ancient Greeks, Avicenna believed that if one of the body's humors was out of balance, then all four of them were unbalanced. As a result, Avicenna and his contemporaries understood cancer to be an extremely difficult disease to treat. He said a benign tumor could be differentiated from a cancerous one by certain symptoms such as pain, throbbing, and rapid growth. He also noted that cancerous tumors send out "crablike tracks" and occurred more often in "hollow" organs, which is why they were more common in women. Avicenna also stated that cancers often strike muscles, tendons, and lymph nodes.

He said a cure was most likely if the cancer was caught at its earliest stages. The first goal should be to halt the cancerous growth. Avicenna recommended surgical removal if the tumor was small and accessible, and not close to major organs. If it "can be arrested with anything, it can be so by vigorous excision . . . including all the [blood] vessels supplying the tumor so that nothing of these will be left." He also advised that surgery be preceded by purifying the body of excess black bile. This could be achieved by providing a nutritious and balanced diet to the patient to maintain purity and strengthen his or her organs and immune system. Avicenna most often treated cancer patients with drug remedies. He also advised cancer patients to change their diets. In advanced cases, Avicenna advised against excision, saying the tumor would only grow back.

Avicenna described meningitis, and he devoted attention to gynecological problems and to proper child care. He performed surgeries and is said to have worn green robes while operating. He also developed surgical instruments, including a probe for the eye.

LIFE IN HAMADAN

After falling out of favor in Rayy, Avicenna made his way to Hamadan, where he was eventually summoned to the court of Prince Shams al-Dawla to treat him for colic. He stayed in the palace for forty days, earning the gratitude and favor of the prince, who gave him a position at his court.

The philosopher accompanied the prince on his military campaigns, as an adviser and physician, and he was soon given the post of vizier, or prime minister.

But the army turned against him (al-Juzjani hinted that the soldiers thought Avicenna might expose their corruption). In a sort of mini coup, the soldiers surrounded his house, hauled him off to prison, and ransacked his belongings. They even tried to get him executed, but the sultan hesitated, instead banishing him from Hamadan. Avicenna instead remained in Hamadan, hiding at the home of a friend.

However, the prince fell ill again, and summoned Avicenna, whose medical skills returned the prince to favorable health. "The emir apologized to him profusely . . . as a

Anatomical drawings of the heart, ear, brain, lungs, and other body parts are visible in this page from an eleventh-century copy of Avicenna's *Canon of Medicine*. Although it was extremely rare for Muslims to dissect the human body, Avicenna learned a great deal about anatomy from Galen, the Greco-Roman physician. Galen had frequently dissected pigs (because their organs most closely resembled that of a human) and monkeys, and was familiar with human anatomy because he served as the chief physician to the Roman gladiators. Both Muslims and Roman Christians considered the dissection of dead human bodies sacrilegious.

result he continued in honor and high consideration at court, and was appointed vizier for a second time," wrote al-Juzjani.

Around the same time, al-Juzjani had been pleading with Avicenna to write a commentary on Aristotle, but the philosopher, who was busy with matters of state, said he didn't have the time. Finally, Avicenna agreed, saying, "If you will be satisfied for me to compose a book setting forth the parts of those sciences which I believe to be sound, not disputing therein with any opponents no troubling to reply to their arguments, I will gladly do so." And that was how he began work on the *Book of Healing* (*Kitab al-Shifa*).

Avicenna was man of great energy and purpose. He rose before dawn for the first prayers of the day, and then wrote for several hours. Later, when his pupils joined him, he discussed his recent passages with them. After a brief period of study, Avicenna began his duties as vizier where he dealt with administrative matters until noon.

He then returned home for lunch, at which time he usually had guests. After eating and socializing, Avicenna usually took a brief rest and later attended to the prince and his court. Avicenna returned home by sunset, where after dinner, he would have another study session with his students, giving lectures and dictating notes for his books. Al-Juzjani noted in the biography, "Studying was done by night because during the day his attendance upon the [e]mir left him no spare time." In the evening they drank wine and were entertained by court musicians (music was another of Avicenna's passions). Among orthodox Muslims of the time, Avicenna's love of coffee and music provoked consternation, and he was also faulted for his odd hours, active love life, and social schedule.

IN SECLUSION

Avicenna's structured court life did not last. After a few years, Prince Shams al-Dawla again fell ill, this time while on a military expedition. His soldiers rushed to bring him back to Avicenna, carrying him in a cradle, but he died on the way. The prince's son, Sama al-Dawla, was installed as emir, and the army asked Avicenna to stay on at his post as vizier. Avicenna refused, however, probably wary of the people who had almost killed him years earlier.

Avicenna went into hiding and wrote to Shams' brother, Ala al-Dawla, emir of Isfahan, seeking a post within his court. In the meantime, at al-Juzjani's prodding, he continued work on his *Book of Healing*. Since he didn't have access to books, he wrote the manuscript entirely from memory. He drew up a framework, and then systematically filled in each topic from a range that included all the natural sciences (except zoology). Al-Juzjani claimed that Avicenna wrote fifty pages every day.

At this time, a search was under way for Avicenna, as the sultan's deputy suspected him of intrigue with Ala al-Dawla.

Betrayed by an enemy, Avicenna was caught and then imprisoned in a fortress called Fardjan where he spent four months. He wrote a couplet, which al-Juzjani quotes in his biography:

My going in was sure, as you have seen
My going out is what many will doubt.

While in prison, Avicenna wrote the *Book of Guidance (Kitab al-Hidaya)*, *The Living Son of the Vigilant (Hayy ibn Yaqzan)*, and a treatise on colic; he had written the *Cardiac Remedies* earlier. As described beforehand, *Hayy ibn Yaqzan* is the tale of a man who grows up alone on an isolated island, yet through sheer intuition, intellect, and reasoning is able to arrive at ultimate truths about reality, being, and God. It is a parable that explains Avicenna's view of knowledge as both intuitive and rational. According to Avicenna, it is through a logical thought process that a connection with the Active Intellect may be formed. This connection is what unveils the mysteries of the universe.

Soon after Avicenna was imprisoned, Ala al-Dawla attacked and captured Hamadan, and Sultan Ali and his minister were placed in the same fortress as Avicenna. Having secured their submission, Ala al-Dawla freed them and allowed Ali to retain nominal authority. Avicenna was released, too, and he took lodgings at the house of a friend.

Chapter 5

DEATH OF AN INTELLECTUAL

Avicenna stayed in Hamadan for a while before heading to Isfahan, to the court of Ala al-Dawla who had won a reputation as a patron of scholars. But Avicenna still feared the vizier, and decided to leave in disguise. He, Abu Ubayid al-Juzjani, his brother, and two slaves disguised themselves as Sufis, Muslim mystics who wore thick woolen robes.

After many hardships, they reached Isfahan. Ala al-Dawla and other notables came out to greet them. "At court he was received with the respect and consideration that he so richly merited," wrote al-Juzjani in his biography of Avicenna.

In this French print, the governor of Isfahan is receiving Avicenna. For most of his life, Avicenna's pursuit of knowledge was a secondary occupation, conducted in his free time. By day he served at the court of various rulers and also ran free clinics through which he practiced medicine. In his later years, he accompanied his sultans on wars and other expeditions. During these times it is said he would write while on horseback, or have a scribe at hand to whom he would dictate his thoughts.

Every Friday night, Ala al-Dawla would gather all the scholars in his court for learned discussions, where Avicenna dazzled his peers and provoked much envy. It was here that the philosopher set about completing the *Book of Healing* and several other works.

KITAB AL-SHIFA

Like the *Canon*, the *Book of Healing* is also an encyclopedia, but it deals mostly with metaphysics, mathematics, astronomy, and the natural sciences.

Avicenna greatly valued the pursuit of knowledge because he believed that it was only through reasoning that humans could perfect their immortal souls. He was convinced that it was only through the pursuit of learning that man could come into contact with the Active Intellect, the tenth celestial entity. For Avicenna, this was the purpose of human life, to experience the divine spark that caused our world. He also believed that knowledge was the sole criterion by which humans would be judged in the afterlife.

Among humans, Avicenna regarded prophets as the most intellectually developed. He believed they had the strongest intuition since they had pure souls and were in contact with the Active Intellect, which enabled them to receive divine revelations.

Since the concepts of metaphysics in the *Book of Healing* were discussed earlier, let's now consider its treatment of the natural sciences. Avicenna believed in both observation and experimentation (which was shunned as impure science by Aristotle). Once, when a meteor fell in the region, Avicenna examined it closely and proceeded to melt it to see whether or not it was metallic. The *Book of Healing* also included detailed descriptions of natural phenomena such as rainbows and geological formations including descriptions of igneous and sedimentary rocks and stalagmites, with references to Avicenna's own childhood observations of the Amu Darya River in Bukhara.

Avicenna devoted special attention to physics and the study of motion, which Aristotle considered the governing principle of the universe. He realized the problems with Aristotle's theory of projectile motion, and theorized a concept of inertia. He also argued that when an object is set into motion, it retains some of that energy, and that energy would not dissipate in a vacuum. Avicenna attempted to calculate this force mathematically, considering that the motion of an object would be inversely proportional to its weight, giving birth to a rudimentary concept of momentum—the product of mass and velocity.

Avicenna also discussed various procedures for purifying metals in the *Book of Healing*. And he rejected the concept of alchemy—the centuries-old hunt for a substance, sometimes called the "philosopher's stone," that would turn ordinary metals into gold. He declared alchemy unscientific and futile and also rejected astrology, writing that it was impossible to say what influence the stars have on our lives.

Avicenna discussed the animal kingdom, focusing mostly on humans. He improved the Aristotelian system by incorporating new information on human anatomy, especially of the female reproductive system and the role of male and female "semen" in reproduction. Aristotle had refused to believe that there were ovaries or female "semen." Avicenna accepted the existence of ovaries, but clung to the incorrect belief that women cannot have more than a passive role in the development of the fetus.

Avicenna also wrote several treatises on the eye, its structure and functioning, and ocular diseases, which were a special concern in the desert lands of Arabia and central Asia. In his discussion of sight, Avicenna breaks with Aristotle, who believed the eye issued some sort of ray toward objects it saw. Instead, he argued that the objects themselves send off rays to the eye. He also argued that sight occurred through the nerves, and not the "crystalline" lens.

As previously mentioned, Avicenna loved music, which was considered a part of mathematics in medieval times. Avicenna's main contributions to math are in the field of music; in fact, he also composed original compositions.

In a short time, Avicenna became one of the sultan's close aides. He held no official position, but he was an esteemed adviser and accompanied the sultan on his journeys and wars. On one such trip, Ala al-Dawla expressed dissatisfaction with astronomical tables and he commissioned Avicenna to update them. Al-Juzjani helped the philosopher select instruments and workers and they proceeded to tabulate more accurate measurements.

It seems from his vast accomplishments that Avicenna was indefatigable. Al-Juzjani narrates an incident in which a messenger brought a note to a pupil of the philosophers' from a certain judge in Shiraz, in southern Persia. The judge objected to some arguments Avicenna had made in an essay on logic that he had incorporated in his *Book of*

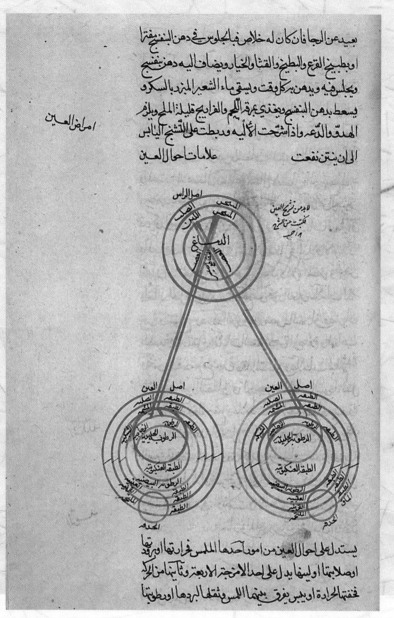

بعيد عن الجلا فان كان له خلاص فيالجلوس في دهن البنفشة او
او بطبيخ القتع والبطيخ والقثاء والخيار ويضاف اليه دهن بنفشج
ويجلس فيه وبدهن بركل وقت ويسقى ماء الشعير المبرد بالسكر
يسعط بدهن البنفشج ويغذى بغمر اللحم والغرابيع قليلة الملح ويلزم
الهدو والدعة واذا استحت الآلية وربطت على التشنج اليابس
الى ان يسكن نفعت   علامات احوال العين

امراض العين

يستدل على احوال العين من امور احدها الملمس فرادتها او بردها
او صلابتها او لينها يدل على احدى الامجزة الاربعة وثانيها من الركة
فخفتها الحرارة او يبس يفرق بينهما الملمس ثقلها البردها او طوبتها

This diagram of the eye was drawn by Ala al-Din Abu al-Hasan Ali ibn Abi al-Hazm al-Qarshi al-Dimashqi al-Misri (ibn al-Nafis) (1213-1288), a Muslim physician who benefited from Avicenna's contributions to medicine. Al-Nafis's greatest accomplishment was the correct understanding of the pulmonary circulation system. He was able to identify and understand the function of the lungs, bronchi, and coronary arteries, 300 years before the Europeans.

Rising to a Challenge

In his biography, Abu Ubayid al-Juzjani narrated an incident that gives us an idea about Avicenna's keen intellect and competitive streak. A question related to philology (the study of literature) arose during a discussion in front of the sultan to which Avicenna also gave his opinion. But one scholar, Abu Mansur al-Jabban, turned to him and said, "You are a philosopher and a wise man, but you have never studied philology to such an extent that we should be pleased to hear you discourse on the subject."

Avicenna was stung by this and devoted the next three years to studying the subject, sending for books from far and wide. When he was satisfied, he composed three odes of rare expression in the style of three different authors. He had the works bound as a book with the title smudged, and presented it to Abu Mansur with the comment, "We found this volume in the desert while hunting, and you must look it through and tell us what it contains."

Abu Mansur examined the book and was baffled by some of the passages. Avicenna then innocently remarked that if he were to read certain books on philology he would understand everything. Abu Mansur then realized that Avicenna was the author and apologized profusely for his prior insults.

Deliverance, or *Kitab al-Najat.* The student handed the note to Avicenna at the end of a long summer day. Avicenna read it and immediately called for ink and paper. While his friends and disciples sat around talking and eventually fell sleep, Avicenna wrote all night, drafting a reply. In the morning, he handed the response, some fifty sheets, to the messenger, saying, "I made haste to reply so that the messenger should not be delayed," wrote al-Juzjani in his biography.

FINAL DAYS

It was with Ala al-Dawla that Avicenna found true respect and support. And in honor of his patron, he composed two works in Persian, which was the sultan's (and Avicenna's) native language.

The more important of these is the *Book of Wisdom for Ala,* or *Danesh-Nama e Alai.* In the preface, Avicenna wishes his benefactor "all his wishes, in security, and eminence and honor" and notes that in this "prince's shadow I have achieved all ambition—for security, dignity, respect for science."

A student of Avicenna's added this diagram to a later edition of the *Canon of Medicine.* It instructs physicians on how to determine a patient's pulse. This copy was created in the seventeenth century.

The *Danesh-Nama* is a concise primer on philosophy, written for a layperson, that includes sections about logic, metaphysics, math, and science. Experts have remarked on its graceful conversational style, its humor and wit, and the ease with which Avicenna transfers complex ideas and terms from Arabic to lively, colloquial Persian.

But alas, Avicenna's final days were less than peaceful. Sultan Mahmud, who had been the scourge of the Abbasids, was again flexing his muscle in Transoxania. Al-Saiyyida of Rayy had died and her son, Majid al-Dawla, finally had his chance on the throne. Unfortunately, he proved an inept ruler and invited Mahmud to help him in his battle with a neighbor. The Ghaznavids took the opportunity to seize Rayy and unleashed a wave of persecution against various sects and ethnic groups.

Ala al-Dawla tried his best to placate Mahmud, but Mahmud eventually sent his son to attack Isfahan in 1030. Ala al-Dawla fled when the Turkish army entered the city, and Avicenna likely left with him. His home in Isfahan was looted and his books were taken to Ghazna. Many of his works were lost forever, including the *Book of Impartial Judgment* (*Kitab al-Insaf*) of which only fragments survive.

It was during this time that Avicenna fell ill with colic. It was a severe attack, and he gave himself strong medicines. To make matters worse, he was on the road with the sultan, fleeing the Ghaznavid army. He gave himself injections, but one of his servants may have given him an overdose of a medicine that made his illness worse. Al-Juzjani hinted that the servants may have attempted to poison Avicenna on purpose, possibly because the servants had stolen from him. Avicenna

In this illustration from the *Compendium of Chronicles* by Rashid al-Din (1247-1318), Mahmud is seen with the Ghaznavid army defeating Baktuzan in one of the last battles on which Avicenna would accompany the sultan. This is one of only two surviving copies of the *Compendium* in Persian. The entire work was created to retell the history of the Mongol peoples in Asia.

was taken back to Isfahan where his condition stabilized enough for him to continue to accompany Ala al-Dawla in battle again. Soon, however, Avicenna's condition deteriorated again and he stopped treating himself, saying to al-Juzjani, "The manager who used to manage me, is incapable of managing me any longer so there is no use trying to cure my illness," as al-Juzjani recounted in his biography. Avicenna died soon after in Hamadan, in 1037, at the age of fifty-seven. He had always said, "I [prefer] a short life with width to a narrow one with length," according to M. A. Martin in *Genius of Arab Civilization*.

Avicenna's contributions to medicine, philosophy, and literature are felt to this day, and modern medical students continue to read his works. This title page *(above)* of *The Book of the Excellent Galen on Medical Sects for Students,* shows Avicenna's annotation on the right, under the main heading he wrote that he "came into possession of the book in 407." This nineteenth-century lithograph portrait of Avicenna *(right)* as a mature man is by a Spanish artist.

Avicenna was not a particularly popular man in his own lifetime. Although he was a devout Muslim, he lived an unconventional lifestyle and had many unconventional views. He never married but was certainly not celibate. Many of his works went against the mainstream Muslim religious thinking at the time and he was often accused of being a *kafir*, or an unbeliever. Allegations of being a closet Shiite followed him his entire life. Seyyed Hossein Nasr writes that Avicenna composed a verse defending himself, "If I am a heretic, then there is not a single Muslim anywhere in the world."

By many historical accounts, Avicenna was of striking good looks. He wasn't falsely modest; he could be arrogant and scornful of mediocre intellects, sometimes ridiculing others' scholarly work.

Throughout history, critics have sometimes spread derogatory rumors about Avicenna; he was even occasionally portrayed after his death as an evil sorcerer. His detractors also liked remarking that the great physician was unable to heal himself. Nonetheless, Avicenna continues to have an impact on science and philosophy today.

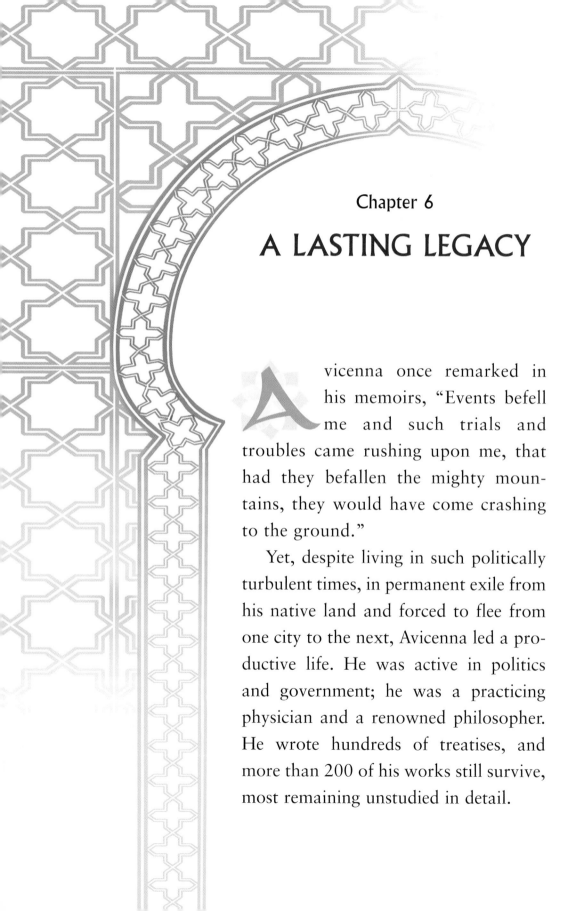

Chapter 6

A LASTING LEGACY

A vicenna once remarked in his memoirs, "Events befell me and such trials and troubles came rushing upon me, that had they befallen the mighty mountains, they would have come crashing to the ground."

Yet, despite living in such politically turbulent times, in permanent exile from his native land and forced to flee from one city to the next, Avicenna led a productive life. He was active in politics and government; he was a practicing physician and a renowned philosopher. He wrote hundreds of treatises, and more than 200 of his works still survive, most remaining unstudied in detail.

·GALENVS ⁖ AVICENA ⁖ VPOCRATES

In the west, Avicenna was regarded as the "prince of physicians," and his images are found in paintings, tapestries, and stained glass windows of many cathedrals and universities. Even the staunch Christian Dante Alighieri gives him a place of honor in his epic poem, *The Divine Comedy*, placing him with Hippocrates *(right)* and Galen *(left)* in the first level of hell, with virtuous souls who were not Christian.

In his lifetime, Avicenna had a mixed reception. For many philosophers who worked within the Greek tradition, Avicenna was a great commentator and elucidator of Aristotelian thought. He provided Muslim, Christian, and Jewish scholars a means to adapt the rationalist Greek methodology to their monotheistic faiths. For physicians, he was the final word, and for philosophers, a foundation on which to build their theories.

But traditional religious theologians, both Christian and Muslim, sometimes rejected Avicenna. They believed that he was an unbeliever because he had adopted pagan Greek logic and appeared to limit God's powers. The notion that Greek-inspired metaphysics, and even sciences, were ungodly was beginning to strengthen, and several caliphs and Christian kings banned or executed philosophers who embraced rational, scientific thought over religion.

In the East, the Abbasid dynasty was fragmenting, and traditionalism and rigidity were taking hold in Arab lands that had once been the centers of experimental learning. Even in faraway Spain, where Muslim rulers had created a cosmopolitan haven for scientists and philosophers, Spanish Christian attacks were taking their toll.

Ironically, in the Muslim territories, Avicenna's metaphysical theories were ultimately eroded because of the criticisms of two philosophers, both schooled in the Greek tradition, but with opposing views.

COHERENCE AND INCOHERENCE

Nearly fifty years after Avicenna's death, Abu Hamid al-Ghazali took issue with the Greek-influenced Muslim philosophers. Since Avicenna was the most important thinker of this group, al-Ghazali focused his study and criticism on Avicenna's work.

What is unique about al-Ghazali's critique is that because he was trained in Greek logic and methods, his analysis is a rational examination of what he thought were the contradictions in Avicenna's metaphysical system. In his *Incoherence of the Philosophers*, al-Ghazali listed twenty features of the *falasifa*'s (philosopher's) thought, of which only three went against both religion and logic. In fact, al-Ghazali felt that the philosophers, in their eagerness to adopt Aristotle, had rejected or mangled parts of their religion that they needn't have.

The first contradiction, according to al-Ghazali, is the falasifa's belief that the universe is eternal, emanating instantaneously from God's self-reflection. Al-Ghazali challenged the belief that if God is logically the only Necessary Being, the universe had to come after him, both in time and being, and therefore cannot be truly eternal. Second, al-Ghazali disagreed with Avicenna's belief that God only governs the universe's, not individual human's, actions. He says there is no contradiction in accepting God's knowledge of all details. Finally, al-Ghazali disagreed with Avicenna's rejection of bodily resurrection, arguing that since God is the Necessary Cause, it is not impossible for him to give bodies to the resurrected souls in the afterlife.

Almost a century later, another great philosopher Abu al-Walid ibn Rushd, known in the West as Averroes, took issue with al-Ghazali, and also with Avicenna. In his response to al-Ghazali, which he titled, *Incoherence of the Incoherence*, Averroes argued that there was no incompatibility between religion and philosophy if both were understood soundly. By that time, Averroes had access to better translations of the Greek works and he blamed the confusion about the apparent contradictions between Aristotle and Islam on Avicenna, saying that the latter had misrepresented the Greeks' thought in his attempt to mesh religion and reason.

At the same time, Averroes admired Avicenna's contributions to medicine, and wrote a book examining a poem Avicenna had crafted, the "Urjuza fi'l-Tibb" ("Poem on Medicine"), which served as a memory aid to students of the *Canon of Medicine*.

Despite criticisms, Avicenna remains a respected figure in the Arabic-speaking world for his accomplishments in both medicine and philosophy. He is called the Sheikh al Rais (Chief of the Wise, or Third Teacher), after Aristotle and al-Farabi.

INFLUENCE IN THE WEST

At the turn of the millennium, as Europeans conquered parts of Muslim Spain, they came into contact with the

Avicenna's *Canon of Medicine* continued to be among the most influential medical texts, long after Avicenna himself had died in 1037. This copy of the *Canon*, translated from Persian into Latin by Gerard of Cremona (1114–1187), one of the most celebrated European translators of Arabic and Persian texts, was completed in miniature, a popular size in medieval Europe.

works of al-Farabi, Avicenna, Averroes, and others, and through them the works of Aristotle and Plato. When the city of Toledo was captured in 1085, they found a translation bureau similar to the Bayt al-Hikma, where multilingual Christian, Jewish, and Muslim scholars were working together to translate books into Hebrew and Latin. Arabic was the international language of science and philosophy at the time.

In the Christian world, the church had mostly banned the study of the Greeks, regarding them as pagans, and the original works written in Greek were lost. But the Arab efforts, especially Avicenna's, to adapt and reconcile Greek thought within a religious framework opened the door for a new Western interest in Aristotle and the other Greek philosophers. This eventually led to the Renaissance and the Enlightenment. As George Rafael, who writes extensively on literature and art, has noted, the "Arabs were midwives to the European Renaissance."

The new Christian rulers took over the bureau in Toledo and began translating the Arabic works into Latin. Many Europeans learned Arabic in order to read the translations of Aristotle and others as well as the falasifa's commentaries and the new medical and scientific treatises. Jewish scholars who had found peace and security in Muslim lands were at the forefront of this work, playing the role the Syrian Christians had played three centuries previously around Baghdad.

One of the most influential Western translators was Gerard of Cremona. Known as the Master, Gerard translated seventy-one works from Arabic, including translations of Avicenna's *Canon*.

The *Canon* soon became the standard textbook throughout Europe. The oldest existing Western syllabus, at the famous School of Medicine at Montpellier in France, lists the *Canon*. The text continued to be used well into the seventeenth century. Medical students learned Arabic in order to study it.

Eventually, of course, medical advances made many aspects of the *Canon* outdated. But as pharmacologist and author N. A. Darmani has noted, "With the composition of the *Canon*, Avicenna placed the keystone in the arch that bridges the medical system of Hippocrates [and] Galen . . . with modern medicine."

In the field of philosophy, Avicenna's metaphysics were to have a profound effect on the medieval Scholastics— Christian theologians who, freshly exposed to Aristotle and Plato, took on the same task as the Muslim falasifa, to reconcile reason with faith. The most important of these scholars, St. Thomas Aquinas, used Avicenna's arguments to build his own rational proof of the existence of God.

Aquinas accepted Avicenna's distinction between essence and existence and the concept of necessary and being. But Aquinas further developed the concept of a theory of causal relationships that better fit with rational science. Aquinas

Avicenna is seen with his students in this contemporary postage stamp from the Republic of Mali. The contributions made by Avicenna and other Muslim physicians, scientists, and philosophers are continually celebrated around the world. Avicenna will never be forgotten. He is so celebrated, in fact, that there is a crater on Earth's moon named in his honor.

disagreed with Avicenna's attempt to prove that the universe was both created and eternal, saying that though it was possible, it was impossible to prove it.

During this time, Avicenna's philosophical reputation was tarnished when some other writers' works were wrongly attributed to him and some of his own works were poorly translated. During this time, the rumblings of the Renaissance were becoming stronger. Leonardo da Vinci rejected the *Canon*, finding it outdated in the natural sciences, but he still used the Arabic terms, since there was no other terminology at the time.

Avicenna's influence, both in the West and East, has survived many interpretations. Scholars today, both in the West and in the Muslim lands, continue to review Avicenna's works, many of which have not yet been subjected to a detailed examination. His medical treatises, especially on herbal cures, still guide natural healers, and his philosophical treatises still help illuminate man's most puzzling questions.

Avicenna is revered as one of the greatest minds of all time—a man with unlimited interests, an insatiable curiosity, and deep, profound appreciation of the mystery of life.

Today's physicists are still in search of a "unified theory," something that will encompass the workings of all natural forces and give them a clue to the origin of the universe. In a sense, Avicenna sought to do the same, as he was looking for a way to understand the universe based on concrete laws of cause and effect, and a wise, loving God. He said in his memoirs, "The heart of learning is a direct insight into the rational principles on which the world is constructed."

TIMELINE

476

Year given by historians to signify the end of the Roman Empire.

570

Birth of the prophet Muhammad in Mecca (Makkah).

610

Muhammad receives the first revelations.

632

Muhammad dies.

660

Muslim armies conquer Egypt and Persia.

661

Muslims split into Shia and Sunni sects.

698

Muslim armies conquer North Africa.

719

The Iberian Pennisula is under Muslim control.

750

The Umayyad dynasty is overthrown by the Abbasid dynasty; Abbasid capital is moved to Baghdad.

760

Arab scholars adopt Indian number system.

768

Unification of the Roman Empire under Charlemagne.

786

Reign of the fourth Abbasid caliph Harun ar-Rashid.

830

The House of Wisdom is built in Baghdad.

980

Avicenna (Ibn Sina) is born in Persia.

998

Avicenna cures the Samanid sultan of Bukhara, Nuh ibn Mansur.

999

The sultan's library is destroyed by fire. Avicenna flees Bukhara and travels to Gurganj in Khiva (Turkmenistan).

1020

Avicenna is imprisoned in a fortress in Fardjan for four months.

1022

Avicenna leaves Hamadan and travels to Isfahan.

1037

Avicenna becomes ill from colic and dies.

GLOSSARY

abase To lower in rank or office.

alchemy A medieval chemical science that studied the convergence of base metals into gold.

Allah The Arabic term for "God" or "the Only God."

arbitration The act of mediating in order to settle a dispute.

assimilate To take in; to understand.

Byzantine Empire The eastern half of the Roman Empire, which survived for 1,000 years after the fall of Rome. Its name comes from Byzantium, the original name of its capital city Constantinople. It declined when the Islamic Turks captured Constantinople in AD 1453.

caliph The title given to Muhammad's successors. The Umayyad rulers of al-Andalus claimed the title in AD 929, although many Muslims dispute their right to it.

capricious Impulsive, unpredictable.

colic A sharp, acute pain in the abdomen.

colloquial Relating to informal conversation.

coup A brilliant, sudden, or unusual stroke or act.

devout Deeply religious or devoted.

emir The Arabic word for an important noble who ruled a large region; it could mean "governor," but it is probably best to translate it as "prince"; also spelled "amir."

Enlightenment A philosophical movement of the eighteenth century that rejected traditional religious, political, and social ideas and ushered in an era of rationalism.

excommunicate To exclude from membership in a church by a religious authority.

exile Forced or voluntary removal from one's kingdom.

extrapolation The inference of unknown information from known information.

heretic A person who holds different religious beliefs from those that are established and widely accepted.

indefatigable Untiring; tireless.

inertia The tendency of a body to remain at rest or continue in motion unless it is disturbed by another force.

Islam The Muslim religion, which includes faith in Muhammad as the prophet of God, or Allah.

jurisprudence The science or philosophy of law.

Kaaba The large, black, cube-shaped shrine in Mecca; the holiest Islamic shrine.

Mecca (Makkah) A city in central Arabia, the birthplace of Muhammad, and the holiest place in the Muslim territories; all Muslims are supposed to pray in its direction five times a day.

metaphysics The nature of reality and being.

methodology A system of principles and procedures applied to a science or discipline.

Moors The name given by the Spanish to the Berber people of North Africa.

mosque A Muslim house of worship.

Muslim A follower of Islam.

opulent Abundant, lavish.

pagan A person who worships many gods.

Persia An ancient empire in the Middle East that occupied the region now called Iran.

premise A proposition upon which an argument is based or from which a conclusion is drawn.

prodigy A child with exceptional talent.

profound Extending to or coming from a great depth; deep.

Shia A large sect of Muslims that separated from the Sunnis after the assassination of Ali. Shia Muslims constitute the majority in present-day Iraq and Iran.

sultan Ruler of a Muslim country.

Sunni The largest sect of Islam. Sunni Muslims reject the Shiite claim that Ali was the rightful successor to Muhammad. Most Arab and African Muslims are Sunni.

syllabus The summary that describes the content taught and the texts used during a university class.

syllogism A formal argument consisting of a major premise and a minor premise leading to a conclusion.

Syriac A language based on Aramaic and used by Christians.

Umayyad A dynasty of caliphs that ruled the Muslim territories until AD 750.

vassal A person in a subordinate social position.

FOR MORE INFORMATION

Islamic Society of North America
6555 South 750 East
Plainfield, IN 46168
(317)839-8157
http://www.isna.net

U.S. National Library of Medicine
History of Medicine Division
Building 38, Room 1E-21
8600 Rockville Pike
Bethesda, MD 20894
e-mail: hmdref@nlm.nih.gov (Reference Librarian)
(301) 402-8878
Web site: http://www.nlm.nih.gov

WEB SITES

Due to the changing nature of Internet links, the Rosen Publishing Group, Inc., has developed an online list of Web sites related to the subject of this book. This site is updated regularly. Please use this link to access the list:

http://www.rosenlinks.com/gmps/avic

FOR FURTHER READING

Haddad, Sami I. *History of Arab Medicine*. Beirut, Lebanon: Oriental Hospital, 1975.

Hayes, John, ed. *The Genius of Arab Civilization*. Cambridge, MA: MIT Press, 1983.

Ispahany, Batool, trans. *Islamic Medical Wisdom: The Tibb al-A'imm*. London, England: The Muhammadi Trust, 1991.

Menocal, Maria Rosa. *Ornament of the World: How Muslims, Jews and Christians Created a Culture of Tolerance in Medieval Spain*. New York, NY: Little, Brown and Company, 2002.

Nasr, Seyyed Hossein. *Science and Civilization in Islam*. New York, NY: New American Library, 1968.

Shah-Kazemi, Reza. *Avicenna, Prince of Physicians*. Washington, DC: Amideast Publications, 1997.

Siraisi, Nancy G. *Avicenna in Renaissance Italy: The Canon and Medical Teaching in Italian Universities After 1500*. Princeton, NJ: Princeton University Press, 1987.

BIBLIOGRAPHY

Arberry, A. J. *Avicenna on Theology.* Westport, CT: Hyperion Press, 1979.

Bearman, P.J., et al., ed. *Encyclopaedia of Islam.* "Ibn Sina." Leiden, Netherlands: Brill Academic Publishers, 2000.

Berjak, Rafik, and Muzaffar Iqbal. *"Ibn Sina: Al-Biruni Correspondence."* Islam and Science, June 2003 (http://www.findarticles.com/p/articles/mi_m0QYQ/is_1_1/ai_n6145344).

Carroll, William E. *"Aquinas on Creation and the Metaphysical Foundations of Science."* Notre Dame University. Retrieved December 22, 2004 (http://www.nd.edu/Departments/Maritain/ti98/carroll.htm).

Carroll, William E. "God Physics: From Hawking to Avicenna." Islamic Philosophy Online. Retrieved December 23, 2004 (http://www.muslimphilosophy.com/sina/art/gpa.doc).

Carroll, William E. *"Thomas Aquinas and Big Bang Cosmology."* Notre Dame University. Retrieved December 23, 2004 (http://www.nd.edu/Departments/Maritain/ti/carroll.htm).

Chishti, Hakim G. M. *The Traditional Healer's Handbook: A Classic Guide to the Medicine of Avicenna.* Rochester, VT: Healing Arts Press, 1988.

Dunn, Peter M. "Avicenna (AD 980–1037) and Arabic Perinatal Medicine." *Archives of Disease in Childhood Online*, July 1997. Retrieved January 3, 2005 (http://fn.bmjjournals.com/cgi/content/full/77/1/F75).

Encyclopædia Britannica Online. "Arts, Islamic." Retrieved January 30, 2005 (http://search.eb.com/eb/article?tocId=13717).

Encyclopædia Britannica Online. "Avicenna." Retrieved November 22, 2004 (http://search.eb.com/eb/article?tocId=9011433).

Encyclopædia Britannica Online. "Kalam." Retrieved December 20, 2004 (http://search.eb.com/eb/article?tocId=9044375).

Encyclopædia Britannica Online. "Kindi, Ya'qub ibn Ishaq as-Sabah, al-." Retrieved December 20, 2004 (http://search.eb.com/eb/article?tocId=9045485).

Encyclopædia Britannica Online. "Logic." Retrieved November 22, 2004 (http://search.eb.com/eb/article?tocId=9110686).

Encyclopædia Britannica Online. "Metaphysics." Retrieved December 20, 2004 (http://search.eb.com/eb/article?tocId=9108718).

Fakhry, Majid. *A History of Islamic Philosophy*. New York, NY: Columbia University Press, 1983.

Gohlman, William E. *Life of Ibn Sina*. New York, NY: State University of New York, 1974.

Goodman, L. E. *Avicenna*. London, England: Routledge, 1995.

Hayes, John, ed. *The Genius of Arab Civilization.* Cambridge, MA: MIT Press, 1983.

Hourani, Albert. *A History of the Arab Peoples.* New York, NY: Warner Books, 1992.

Houser, Rollen E. "Avicenna, Aliqui, and the Thomistic Doctrine of Creation." Retrieved December 28, 2004 (http://www. stthom.edu/houser/avicenna2000.pdf).

Leaman, Oliver. "Islamic philosophy." *Routledge Encyclopedia of Philosophy.* E. Craig, ed. London, England: Routledge. Retrieved February 27, 2005 (http://www.rep.routledge.com/article/H057).

Marmura, Michael E. "Avicenna on Causal Priority." *Islamic Philosophy and Mysticism.* Parviz Morewedge, ed. New York, NY: Caravan Books, 1981. Retrieved January 3, 2005 (http://www.muslimphilosophy.com/sina/art/marmura4.pdf).

Nasr, Seyyed Hossein. *Science and Civilization in Islam.* New York, NY: New American Library, 1968.

Nasr, Seyyed Hossein. *Three Muslim Sages.* New York, NY: Caravan Books, 1976.

Rafael, George. "A Is for Arabs." Salon.com. Retrieved December 28, 2004 (http://www.salon.com/books/feature/2002/01/08/alphabet/index.html).

Sharif, M. M., ed. *A History of Muslim Philosophy.* Lahore, Pakistan: Pakistan Philosophical Congress, 1961. Retrieved January 3, 2005 (http://www.muslimphilosophy.com/hmp/default.htm).

Whitaker, Brian. "Centuries in the House of Wisdom."
    Guardian, September 23, 2004. Retrieved December 28,
    2004 (http://www.guardian.co.uk/life/feature/
    story/0,13026,1310285,00.html).

Wickens, G. M. *Avicenna: Scientist and Philosopher, a
    Millenary Symposium*. London, England: Luzac and
    Co., 1952.

Winter, H. J. J. *The Life and Thought of Avicenna*.
    Bangalore, India: Indian Institute of Culture, 1952.

Yarshater, Ehsan, ed. "Avicenna." *Encyclopedia Iranica*.
    New York, NY: Routledge, 1982.

INDEX

About the Author

Aisha Khan is a journalist from India who is now based in Los Angeles, California, where she lives with her husband and daughter. From a family of booklovers, she was exposed early on in her father's library to the rich scientific and philosophical traditions in Islam. This sparked an abiding interest in the Middle East and Central Asia, which she pursued in graduate school at New York University.

About the Consultant

Munir A. Shaikh, Executive Director of the Council on Islamic Education (CIE), reviewed this book. CIE is a non-advocacy, academic research institute that provides consulting services and academic resources related to teaching about world history and world religions. http://www.cie.org.

Photo Credits

Cover Bibliotheque de la Faculte de Medecine, Paris, France, Archives Charmet/ Bridgeman Art Library; pp. 7, 81, 83 Courtesy National Library of Medicine; p. 10 Bibliotheque Nationale, Paris, France/Bridgeman Art Library; pp. 13, 35 Map by András Bereznay, http://www.historyonmaps.com; p. 15 Bridgeman-Giraudon/ Art Resource, NY; p. 18 The New York Public Library/Art Resource, NY; p. 21 The Art Archive/Hazem Palace Damascus, Syria/Dagli Orti; p. 24 Snark/Art Resource, NY; pp. 26, 56, 70, 82 background tiles courtesy of Mosaic House, New York; pp. 29, 69 ©SSPL/The Image Works; p. 32 Kalyan Mosque, Bukhara, Uzbekistan/Bridgeman Art Library; p. 37 Topkapi Palace Museum, Istanbul, Turkey/Bridgeman Art Library; p. 41 Scala/Art Resource, NY; pp. 42, 93 Bibliothèque nationale de France; p. 46 Freer Gallery of Art, Smithsonian Institution, Washington, D.C.: Gift of Charles Lang Freer, F1923.5; p. 50 © The British Library, Shelfmark Or. 12208, f.298; pp. 55, 89 © Bettmann/Corbis; p. 57 Erich Lessing/Art Resource, NY; p. 59 © 2004 Werner Forman/TopFoto/The Image Works; pp. 63, 66 Wellcome Library, London, England; p. 72 The Art Archive/National Museum Damascus, Syria/Dagli Orti; p. 77 © Mary Evans Picture Library/The Image Works; p. 85 Used with permission of Edinburgh University Library [Or Ms. 20. f. 120r]; p. 86 (top) The Granger Collection, New York; p. 86 (bottom) Museo Real Academia de Medicina, Madrid, Spain/ Bridgeman Art Library; p. 96 1980 stamp, The Republic of Mali.

Designer: Les Kanturek; Editor: Joann Jovinelly
Photo Researcher: Gabriel Caplan